There Is An Urgency

A Memoir

Gregrhi Love

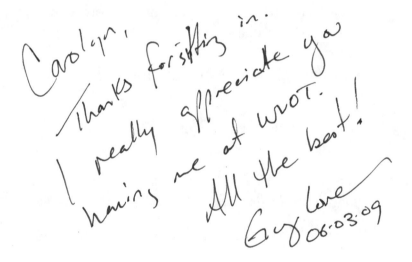

Cwn Annwn Publishing

Murfreesboro, Tennessee

Printed in the United States of America

Library of Congress Cataloging-in-Publication

Data is available.

ISBN-13: 978-0-9823074-0-3

Dedication

I would like to dedicate this book to all of my family and friends, near and far: to my mother Marie Love for her unconditional love and support, my father James Love who taught me how to be a man, to my sisters and brothers for their support, encouragement and infinitely distracting good times, to Karen Jones for her love, patience and support throughout the writing of this book, and finally to Charles Patrick for helping keep me sane all these years in Tennessee.

Acknowledgments

I need to thank all my family and friends who donated money, time, and talent to make this book possible. I need to acknowledge my partners in Write Club and Tracy Cabanis for making me seek and find the hope that shaped this book into what it is. I would also like to acknowledge the unwavering support and encouragement of my family, friends, colleagues and students.

Preface

I lie a lot. I lie about my name, my family, my
past and who I am. I lie to protect myself from
my emotions and my weaknesses. I lie to hide the
shame that keeps me from the normal life that I
crave so desperately. Now, anxiety makes me feel
as if I may die at any time, and I must get the
truth out before it destroys me.

I was thirty before I would admit to any of these
things ever happening. I had always denied that
there was any sort of sexual abuse and had always
downplayed the severity of the physical abuse that
I would admit to. Denial served me well
throughout the years of in- and outpatient
psychiatric care.

In the winter of 2003, the important relationships
in my life seemed destined to fail without some
sort of intervention. Those invaluable
relationships with friends and family kept me
tethered to this fragile life. In a personally
shocking moment of honesty I sat my mother

down at her kitchen table and detailed far too many experiences that she probably would have been happy not to know. However, unlike many people, I was able to choose my family. So, while I opened myself up to more questions than I might have felt comfortable answering, there was a sacred safety and compassion at that table. Moreover I knew, without question, that there would be no judgment.

There is no freedom or escape from the horrors of my early life. Only now there is an urgency to share these experiences and make others aware that people like me walk among us every day. The constant struggles to relate and assimilate, the social phobias and anxiety are all the result of situations I did not instigate and could never have prevented. My personality and frame of reference are deeply rooted in circumstances that should have killed me. In the past I have often wished they had.

Most of the people with whom I take issue in this writing are dead or on their way there. The people that are still alive don't know or wouldn't believe that I am. In this writing certain names and identifying characteristics have been changed to protect the identities of children and their families. The names of most the adults have not been changed. So now, I must start at the beginning.

On Saturday, November 10, 1973, I was born to Debbie, a twenty-three-year-old prostitute and drug addict. My biological father, Howard, was a twenty-four-year-old addict and Vietnam vet. He says he was in and out of my life as a child, but court records show that he was consistently in and out of prison during my childhood. With Howard in prison, the only father figure I remember as a child was Robert W. II, whom I alternately called Bobby and Dad, depending on his mood. He was Debbie's pimp, primary drug supplier, and the father of two of her children.

My first known address was 86 Pequonnock
Street in Bridgeport, Connecticut. Like
everywhere I lived during those years, it is within
walking distance of downtown Bridgeport.
Childhood amnesia has wiped out any memory of
86 Pequonnock. From recently obtained medical
records, I know that I fractured my skull in the
apartment when I was nine months old. Debbie
reportedly sat me on the toilet and I fell off,
hitting my head on the bowl – or so was her story
according to hospital records. It was two days
before she took me to the hospital. The records
report substantial suspicion of child abuse and
neglect. The Department of Children's Services
became an active part of my life in 1974.
The address I remember most clearly was
Building 38, Apartment 304 in Bridgeport's
Father Panik Village. At the time, Father Panik
Village was the second largest housing project in
the Northeast and the sixth largest in the country
- a desolate war zone paved building to building

with concrete. When I lived there, the Village had a total of 1,063 tiny apartments within 44 buildings on 40-acres on the east side of Bridgeport. Through no fault of my own, the Village began to fall into disrepair in the 1970's. I attended school directly across the street from the Village with all of the other project kids. School and especially its library were my sanctuary on the days I attended.

Debbie died a slow and painful death as a result of a lifetime of drug addiction and a desperately hard lifestyle. She was in her late forties when she finally died, nearly five years after I last saw her. When I found her she was in the same hospital I was born in and the same hospital where I had spent a lot of time when I was her child. As she lay there in her bed emaciated and pale, I felt no connection, no sadness, and, surprisingly, no anger. All I wanted were answers to questions that had robbed me of sleep and peace for years and years. All I got were the incoherent

ramblings of a drug fiend. I wanted to find Bobby. I was an adult now, and I had something for him, but I also wanted to find Howard. In the end, I found them both. Strangely, I decided to leave Bobby alone.

I met my biological father in August 1995. Through prison and military records, I was able to get his phone number, and I called him cold one morning. Our only meeting took place shortly after that in another public housing facility in Bridgeport. I met him at his mother's apartment and couldn't get away fast enough. Already an accomplished cook, I occupied my time critiquing the food they served me. When I finally left, I said I'd be back. The next morning, I drove 1,000 miles to middle Tennessee. I don't think much of or about Howard. I never knew him. There was only ever a curiosity of knowing where I came from. He didn't know where I had been and didn't seem to care much. The few hours we spent together gave me everything I

ever wanted to know and filled the place in me where his memory should have been.

To my deep regret and ultimate sadness, Bobby W. is the only father that I knew as a child. Without question or argument, Bobby was the most evil creature I have ever known. Now, I am forced to come to terms with the deep and irreproachable impact life with Bobby has had on who I am, what I have become, and what I do on a daily and routine basis.

In March of 1980, the Connecticut Department of Social Services placed me in my first foster home under protective custody. While the series of events that transpired in each foster placement were horrifying in their own right, nothing ever compared to the daily near-death experiences I was allowed to survive while living with Bobby and Debbie. My older brother Matthew, born November 11, 1972, toured the foster care system along with me (and one time without me), but was always only along for the ride. His

experiences with Bobby, for some inexplicable reason, were the polar opposite to my own. Years later it would be conjectured that Matthew's own path in life and countless prison sentences were due in large part to the psychological neglect that professionals say he *must* have felt during the years spent living with Bobby and Debbie. When I've asked him, all he ever says is that he likes to get high and that's what gets him in trouble. Alcohol and drugs, he says, are the catalysts for his criminal behavior. He has no negative feelings toward Bobby but has often spoken ill of Debbie. Matthew blames Debbie and me for taking Bobby from him.

Bobby and Debbie had two children together, the oldest, Ruby, briefly accompanied Matthew and me to my first foster home. She was promptly given back to her father as he was deemed fit to keep her since Debbie took the fall for all the abuse. The younger, commonly known as L.B., short for "Little Bobby", is by all accounts his

father's son. I have never met him, seen or spoken to him, except for the picture I was given by a social worker when he was born. I met Ruby in 1995, but only caused her more trouble than she could stand. I only saw her twice before she disappeared. At the time, she was living with her father in Stratford, Connecticut. I had sat outside of their place in my old beat up car and watched Bobby come and go for days at a time. I knew what I wanted to do, and I knew how to do it. I just needed some help. At the time, Matthew was fresh out of prison, and I needed a gun, not to kill, just to get in the door. After months of reconnaissance, I got the call that I needed.

"Two Glocks, no bodies, a hundred bucks," said a voice on the phone.

We quickly arranged a time and a place to meet. At that moment, I knew my life was over. There could be no turning back. As I rested the receiver into the cradle, I pulled the phone back to my ear, "Matt?"

"What?"

"I'm not coming. Don't ever call me again," the phone rocked as it settled into the cradle. I stood still, frozen in the moment.

There was nothing left for me there. I had to get out and break free. Leaving was the only option. At nearly the same time, I got a call from a friend living in Tennessee. He needed some help and I needed a break. I went to his small college town and discovered the perfect hiding place. Shortly after my visit, I hastily applied to the university and decided that if I were accepted, I would move and leave this life behind. Four months after my visit I packed my car and drove all night to my new home and my new life. The life I have created is better than I could have ever envisioned or hoped to achieve.

I have earned a bachelor's and a master's degree in education and have been teaching for close to a decade at this point. I have purposely sought out the most difficult and hard to reach children

to work with, and I have been extremely successful and satisfied in my work. Working with my kids keeps me grounded and allows me to use the experiences of my life to help children who live in a similar world. My experiences, positive and negative, give me a perspective most people do not have and knowledge that cannot be obtained from a textbook or in a classroom. What follows is an abbreviated account of my formative years with alternating chapters describing my professional life and the use of my childhood traumas to change the lives of the youth of today. It is raw and mean and not easy to read, or write. But I must do it without sympathy or sorrow. This is all true, and I know, right now, similar experiences are happening to some child somewhere. It is up to us to first believe that this is true in our society and next to take action.

Chapter One

Juvenile Detention

I stepped onto the block without saying a word. It was my first night in Juvenile Detention. It'd been a long time since I'd been in a detention facility but this time I was working. I followed my Corporal as he took me on a tour of the facility. We stopped in front of the first cell and a few kids yelled out greetings and requests to the Corporal. The stocky teenager in the first cell spoke nervously.

"Yo, Tre man, what'd I do?"

"Hey man, no one said you did anything"

"Then why's he here?" the young man asked pointing at me while backing away from the bars.

"He's with me," was the Corporal's only reply.

"He new?"

"I told you, he's with me."

Then another child's voice called, "Oh shit, that looks like Mr. Love. Hey 15, don't that look like Mr. Love?" There was a face pressed against the

bars in the next cell with the number 14 painted above it. I stood looking into the cell in front of me, cell 13, while the Corporal spoke with the kids. Everyone wanted to know who I was but the Corporal wasn't saying a word about me. I was there to shadow. I had to complete 40 hours of training before interacting with any detainees. By the end of the short six-cell hallway the shouts and warnings from the kids to each other got louder and more ominous. We turned and made our way back to where we had started. I marched confidently behind the Corporal.

As we emerged from the top of the hall, known as a block, the Corporal turned and smiled at me. "These kids seem to know you already. That's good. Let's get to the next block."

"You let the kids call you by your first name?" I asked quickly.

"You'll see a lot of these kids again and again, you'll get to know them and they'll get to know you. The ones that know me call me Tre. It's a

comfort thing. You can have them call you whatever you want. Whenever you feel like talking." He was a young man, obviously well liked and respected by the kids. He smiled and walked on continuing the tour.

We turned a corner and then another, passed the showers and onto the second six-cell block.

With ear piercing volume we were greeted with, "Yo, 24, it IS Mr. Love, ya'll better watch out, he's a mean mother-," the Corporal gave the child a look mid-sentence and the boy stopped, back-peddled and started again, "yo, he's a badass. What's up Mr. Love? You remember me from school?" asked the tall skinny boy in the dark cell. I looked at him sternly, nodded slightly, and moved down the block shadowing the Corporal.

"Don't fuck with Mr. Love, he'll make you do push-ups and shit. Man, I had him in class, he was mean as hell."

"Mr. Love cool though, he keep it real."

"Yo, why you aint talkin'?"

"Man, dude look crazy. He aint sayin shit and he just be starin'. Yo man, dude IS crazy."

All the way down the block the kids shouted to each other and to the Corporal. I kept a stone face and remained silent. I had been in the building for less than an hour, and I didn't know the rules any better than a fish (inmate slang for a new detainee) so I kept my mouth shut. No one told me I couldn't talk but no one had told me what I could say either. Playing it close to the vest I thought it best to keep my mouth closed until I could make an assessment of the situation, which would take some time. I knew I had five eight-hour shifts before I had to do any real work. I could take my time and let the kids talk about who and what they thought I was.

We descended the stairs into the office area below. Officers had brought in several more kids and as I scanned the scene I recognized one of the juveniles. He looked at me with

embarrassment in his eyes and quickly looked at the floor.

""Yo, Love, this how you do a search," the Corporal was addressing me and I took my eyes from my former student.

"Go ahead take off your belt and put it on this desk, man," the Corporal commanded the new detainee as he made a half turn to point out where he wanted the belt placed. When the belt was on the desk he motioned to the young man, "Turn around, put your hands on the door then take a step back." The young man did as he was told, his eyes trained on the ground.

Turning to me as he put on rubber gloves the Corporal began his instructions, "Start with the hair, run your fingers through, feel around for any bobby pins, rubber bands, or whatever might be in the hair. If they got braids they gotta pull 'em out if they're gonna stay. Go around down to the ears, make sure they're not wearing any earrings. Move down to the collar of the shirt,

check the neck for any jewelry. If they're wearing more than one shirt make 'em strip down to the last one and hang the rest up here," he pointed to the corner of an open door.

"Search the sleeves all the way around, get as high up as you can. You wanna make sure they aint got nothing under their shirt. Feel down the back, down the front. Get to the waist, run your hand around the inside of the waistband of the pants. Check for anything that doesn't belong there. Most o' the time the pants are gonna be sagging so you'll find your own way to do it, but you gotta keep their pants up while you search all of the pockets. Make sure you check on the inside of the waistband cuz a lot of these new pants have pockets on the inside. Feel the crotch area, some people have a problem with this part but you gotta get over that cuz you gotta do it. This is where they wanna hide most of their shit. Get right up on it, don't worry about makin them uncomfortable, most of these dudes they been

here before, they know what's up." The Corporal quit talking and patted the kid down quickly. He demonstrated the rest of the search process and together we cleared the room, escorting the kids to a secure holding area.

"So, Mr. Love," the Corporal said with a smirk, "you're a teacher, huh?" he asked.

"Yes Sir." I replied.

"Yo, chill on that. You aint gotta call me 'Sir'. Tre, just Tre. You're like, ten years older than me anyway." His smile and tone were genuine.

"Cool, I was just showing respect. Ya know? You out-rank me, we just met, I didn't wanna disrespect you, man," I threw up my arms, "you know how it goes being the new guy. I'm just easin' into it."

"It's cool," he assured me before turning to the Sergeant. His smile got bigger when he declared, "We needed this guy months ago." He threw his arm back and pointed at me. "We were upstairs and every kid knows him and they're all afraid of

him. He never said a word. It was great." The Sergeant looked up at me from the desk.

"Why do all of the kids know you?" she asked smugly.

"I'm a teacher. I teach in an alternative school outside of Nashville and before that I taught in the alternative school here. I've taught most of those kids up there and the ones I haven't taught know who I am from the kids I have taught."

"What are you doing here if you're a teacher?"

"Student loans are killing me."

"Yeah, but what are you doing HERE if you teach all day? Why get a job at juvenile detention? Why not get a job doing something other than dealing with these fucked up kids when you deal with fucked up kids all day?" her tone was earnest, yet probing. The small office area was filling up with other detention officers, too many people I didn't know. I considered the question and the inquisitor. I let the question hang and I stood up to introduce myself to the

people in the room. Before there were any more questions, or even time to answer the one waiting for an answer, the door buzzer sounded and deputies could be seen waiting outside with more kids.

Everyone in the office jumped into action. The police were buzzed in and the kids lined up. Everyone was suddenly busy with machine-like precision, asking questions of the police officers and the kids, searching and prepping the kids for booking. I was impressed with the speed and orderliness of the operation. Everyone knew their job and jumped to it. I stood in the corner of the office observing the routine. The police left and the kids were hustled along. The rattle of the leg shackles, the constant buzz from the camera monitors, the natter of the kids, known as detainees; in just a few hours all of these new sounds quickly blended into the white noise of the building. I kept myself to myself as I always tell my students to do. I did as I was told and

answered any questions the staff asked as cryptically as possible. The night moved along quickly as I tried to absorb the routine of my new duties, the whole time shadowing Corporal Tre Rubin. At midnight my shift was over and I stepped out the back door of the detention center into the cool night air. An overwhelming sense of anxiety slammed down on me and it occurred to me for the first time in a long time how good it felt to be free.

I drove home with the radio off enjoying the silence. The ride home was short but the entire evening's events played over in my mind. The faces of the children pained my heart and brought my own childhood horrors rushing forward. I pulled into the garage and sat silently in my Jeep collecting my thoughts before going inside. When I opened the door to the house my dog was wagging her tailless rear end in excitement. I stooped down and pressed my face into her and assured myself that I was really free.

I worked Friday and Saturday night and Sunday morning. The weekend passed quickly. I watched, listened, and learned. Kids tried to speak with me but I stared through them in silence. Instead I chose to carefully observe the rapport the other staff had with the detainees, assessing the attitudes of both. For two nights I shadowed Corporal Rubin closely. He didn't work Sundays so the Sergeant on duty trained me. She was as curt as the other Sergeant had been, but she knew her stuff, and she got the job done. At four o'clock I was glad to walk out the back door and breathe my freedom in deeply. Working two jobs made the weekdays fly by. School seemed like a blur the first week. When Friday rolled around again I pulled off my sweater at the end of the school day and absent-mindedly revealed my JDC uniform shirt. One of my students noticed it immediately.

"Mr. Love, Sir, do you work at the Juvenile Detention Center too?"

"Yes Sir I do. I just started last weekend. I work Friday and Saturday from four until midnight and Sunday from 8 until 4 in the afternoon."

The boy who had spoken looked around at the other boys and they all broke out in uneasy laughter. All of my students had been arrested at one time or another and most of them had spent time locked up in the same detention center I was heading to when the bell rang for dismissal. One student spoke out, "Man, I aint ever getting arrested again. I aint spending my weekends with you too."

"For real," came the chorus from the rest of the class.

The bell rang, the boys filed out quietly and I headed to my car, having made an arrangement with my principal to leave as soon as my students had left for the day. I drove to the detention center and found a spot to park in the packed lot. From the look of the lot first shift was still working and it looked like all of the second shift people

had arrived as well. I let myself in the back door and as I approached the secure entrance the door opened and I was face to face with the Lieutenant. He was a jovial and pleasant man. I had only met him a few times during the hiring process, but he seemed nice enough. He said my name like he was singing a song in a deep southern drawl, "Greg Love," he changed his tone but it was still pleasant, "we gotta talk." He motioned for me to follow him into an office area. "Who are you?" he asked with a Cheshire cat grin.

"I'm not sure what you mean, Sir. What do you want to know?" I was sincerely confused. When he hired me there had been some confusion with another Greg Love that had shown up when he did my background check but that had been cleared up when the picture came back and the Greg Love with a criminal history looked nothing like me at all, aside from all of our information

being different. My face contorted and I waited for his response.

"Man," he began in the same sing song tone he had before, "I been hearin your name all week. 'Mr. Love, Mr. Love, Mr. Love', you have every kid in this place talkin'. These boys have done nothin' all week but ask everyone about you and if you really work here. What I get from the kids is that every one of them is afraid of you. Now I need to know who you are and if you're gonna be a liability." He smiled but I felt his solemnity.

"Sir, I'm just a teacher." I started in but he held up his hand and interrupted.

"Man, stop this 'Sir' shit, Antwan, my name's Antwan, call me Antwan."

"Yes Sir, like I told you before, I know a lot of these kids or I know their families. I've been in a lot of their homes. I do a lot of home visits and I get involved in their lives beyond school. I take my job very seriously and when kids screw up at school I go to their houses and speak with their

folks or whoever takes care of them at home. I
don't play when it comes to school and
discipline." I found myself getting nervous and I
began to sweat as I defended myself.

"You ever hit a kid?"

"No Sir!" I replied without hesitation.

"You sure?" he asked again.

"Yes Sir!" angrily this time.

"Then why they all so afraid of you?" he asked,
seemingly not understanding my rationale.

Now that I understood what he wanted to know I
instinctively switched to a more confident stance
and tone, "I'm very strict, and I always do what I
say I'm going to do. I have high expectations for
my kids and myself, and I follow through to make
sure we all meet those expectations. When they
don't meet expectations or if they break an
agreement I do whatever I have to do to get
through to my kids, even if that means going to
their house, calling their probation officer, or

even visiting them here, which I've done several times in the past as a teacher."

"Cool, as long as you aint gonna kill anybody. You come in here for one weekend and the whole place is turned upside down talking about you, ya know I had to make sure you were all right. Now you're sure you don't wanna work full-time? Cuz I could use you." He smiled again as I denied his offer.

"All right, Mister Love, you need anything let me know. Your forty hours will be up Saturday night so make sure you're ready to go Sunday morning. They're gonna need your help; we're a little short. You smoke?"

"Sometimes"

"Let's go have a cigarette, then I'm outta here. You sure you don't wanna work full-time?" smiling broadly he put his hand on my back and lead me back the way we came and out the secure door.

The weekend went on without incident and I kept to myself as I had before. Each night I shadowed Tre and became more comfortable with my duties. On Sunday I jumped right in and got to work. I followed the orders I was given and did my best. As I began interacting with the detainees I introduced myself to each child I dealt with.

"Good morning Sir. My name is Mr. Love. You can call me 'Mr. Love' or you can call me 'Sir'. If you need anything let me know."

After one such introduction I began shackling a child to bring him out of his cell when I heard a voice from an adjoining cell that I recognized.

"Excuse me," the voice cracked and the speaker cleared his throat, "Mr. Love, Sir, aint you writing a book about child abuse?

"Yes Sir, I am," I responded politely.

"See I told you I knew him. I was in his class last school year," the kid declared to his cellmate in a snarky tone. "When you're done Sir, can we read

it?" He went on, cementing the notion that he did in fact know me.

"Well, it's pretty rough. It's definitely not appropriate for young people."

"Come on Mr. Love, we already locked up. You the one always telling us to read everything we can."

I smiled; he was using my own argument against me. But before I could answer him a small voice to my left asked, "Sir, are you really writing a book about child abuse?"

"Yes Sir, I am."

"I was abused for a long time. I'm in state's custody now. My parents don't even know I'm here. Do you need to interview people for your book, cuz I'll do it." I looked at the young man, his voice meeker than his appearance would suggest.

"No Sir, I'm not interviewing anyone but if you need to talk my name is Mr. Love, I'll be around."

He smiled shyly and went back to his bunk. I finished shackling the young man I was bringing out and walked to the top of the block to open the cell door. The giant cell keys clanged as I unlocked and opened the large metal lock box that contained the antique levers that operated the cells. Trying to distract myself I thought about the Detention Center, and how it was built in the late 1800's. The cells and their mechanisms had never been updated. The cells operated by ratcheting large levers, one for each cell up and down. The cells moved on an enormous chain-driven track. It was important to make sure no one had their hands on the bars as the force of the cells opening and closing could easily break bone. After releasing the operating lever and closing the heavy lock box door, the young man shuffled into the hall and I realized that, more than ever, I had to finish my book. I had to tell the story.

Chapter Two
Making a Man

The welfare office was across town from the projects. Debbie and I walked there every few weeks to confirm our continued need for services. Even at five years old, Matthew didn't have to go because he was allowed to stay home with Bobby, or alone waiting for Bobby, whenever Debbie and I had to go out. That's how Bobby wanted it. When we arrived at the welfare office, one of the workers saw my blackened, shoeless feet and reprimanded Debbie for my condition. Debbie attempted in vain to defend herself. Declining to argue, the social worker walked away and returned quickly back to my chair with a pair of clean socks and bright new sneakers. She gently massaged them onto my feet. Debbie cried in the office and along the entire walk home. When we got to the block before our building, she made me take off the shoes and socks, which she stuffed in her bag and later presented to Matthew. For

months Matthew wore the name brand shoes with pride. Debbie and I never said a word about how they had been given to me. As usual, Debbie did not mention the encounter at the welfare office to Bobby. Bobby was too proud for welfare, and as long as he was around, he said, we didn't need it. He made all of his money from an array of illegal businesses, but Bobby's absence for days at a time, combined with Debbie's uncontrollable drug habit, left us without money or food, so welfare was our only true means of survival. Today as Debbie and I walked back home, our arms full of bags, I knew I had new shoes I'd be allowed to call my own. Debbie had bought new shoes at the supermarket for Matthew and me. She had let me pick out my own shoes from the bins lining the aisle of the grocery store. I had picked out the cleanest looking pair with the fewest scuffmarks. I sat down on the cold floor in the middle of the aisle and tried them on. The snug fit felt simultaneously like a warm blanket

and a kind embrace. I had spent most of the spring and summer wearing cheap dollar store flip-flops. Each pair was kept until they were completely worn out or broken beyond repair. Much of that summer, like all summers, I had gone barefoot, burning the soles of my feet on the hot asphalt as Debbie and I walked the streets of Bridgeport. Bobby refused to let Debbie spend any money on me specifically. I grew giddy as I thought ahead to the time I would be allowed to wear them. In the meantime, they swung inside one of the bags I lugged back to the apartment. Debbie's keychain jingled as we ascended the dark rancid stairwell with the groceries and, most importantly, our new shoes. She pushed open the thick apartment door with unease. When the door opened without resistance from the chain lock, we both knew immediately that Bobby was not home. When we entered the tiny apartment, I immediately noticed Matthew lying comfortably on the couch watching *Gilligan's Island* on

television. He lay there, silent and unmoving, until at Debbie's suggestion, he got up to help put the groceries away. As we unpacked the bags, he saw the new shoes and instantly started begging to put them on. Reluctantly, Debbie permitted us to put them on, and to our surprise, after more prodding from Matthew, she said we could wear them outside. "Wear them outside," meant I could go outside. Bobby didn't let me out of the apartment often because I was always bruised and cut up and I might talk to someone about what went on inside the apartment. Additionally, when he did allow me outside, I typically attracted a crowd of other children because of my appearance, being white and perpetually bruised. Instantly forgetting the threat of the outdoors, I raced after Matthew as he flung the door open and careened down into the dark stairwell, leaping down the stairs, just careful enough not to touch the graffiti and urine soaked walls. We quickly made it to the bottom floor and exploded

from the door-less entranceway into the sunshine,
where we went our separate ways. Matthew had
friends in the surrounding buildings that he ran
off to play with. I had no friends to run to, so I
ran to the deserted playground alone. Matthew
and I were brothers, but not friends. We were
friendly only in cooperative situations.

Matthew and I had different fathers, and we
knew this early on. We were told that Matthew's
father was dead and mine was in prison. Matthew
was older than me by just under a year; we were
the same age for one day, and that fact made him
very angry. He told me that life had been better
for him before I was born, but he was too young
to remember any of that. He was Bobby's
favorite, and we were often pitted against each
other for Bobby's amusement. When we were
locked in our room for hours at a time, we would
play together out of boredom, but otherwise we
avoided each other.

I ran directly to the abandoned monkey bars that lay between the buildings in clear view of the street and the apartment. From here, I could have some warning of Bobby's return. Reaching the hot tangle of metal, I saw that I had the monkey bars to myself. I immediately climbed to the coveted spot at the top. In later times, I would play "King of the Mountain" on these same bars, but now I was alone and friendless. I swung down onto the bars and reached from bar to bar, enjoying the freedom of the outdoors. Without warning, a loud echo rang inside the monkey bars, and from my inverted angle I saw a pale orange basketball bounce into the air from outside the bars. Now it seemed like my new white shoes had attracted every child from all of the surrounding buildings, though I knew it was me that had attracted them. Scanning the area, I saw no trace of Matthew, and I knew I was on my own. I could hear the familiar song over and over

as the boys approached and circled around beneath me.

BoBos, they make ya feet feel fine,
BoBos, cost a dollar ninety-nine,
BoBos, even the welfare will provide!

A small gang of black and Latino boys rallied in a circle and sang their rhyme over and over, as they taunted me in my new shoes. Being one of only a few white children in the Village, I was a frequent target of attack by the other children.

"Man, you see those shoes, they almost as white as he is," jeered one of the boys, as he slapped my dangling bruised arm. I was hanging upside down when they had approached, and I was trying without much success to pull myself up to a seated position at the top of the monkey bars. My body was sore from the previous day's beating, and I had been enjoying my rare time outside of the apartment. Blinded by the sun, I swung back down to shield my eyes.

Some of the boys had climbed through the monkey bars and began slapping and tugging at my arms. I braced my feet against my thighs, trying to steady myself as I hung upside down. The boys were trying to pull me down, and they held my arms despite my flailing.

"Man look at dis sucker's bobos. You get dem today?" one of the crew chided.

"Yeah, my mom got 'em for me," I announced proudly.

"Yo momma? Yo momma's a hooker. My momma say she seen her hookin' all night," one of the boys accused.

"She's trickin', not hookin'" I retorted, knowing the proper term for what my mother did for Bobby.

"What da shit, yo momma a magician with her tricks?" The boys laughed as they made mock magic trick gestures in the air.

"No, she *turns* tricks, that's what it's called, not hookin." I was indignant and not willing to back

down when these boys didn't even know what tricks were. Momentarily I thought I had the upper hand, as the boys looked at me in disbelief. I was wrong.

"And yo daddy her pimp!" someone exclaimed, and the gang began laughing harder.

"And a thief," another boy interjected through his laughter.

"He's not my daddy!" I screamed, still trying to keep my legs wrapped around the thin steel bar I hung from.

"You aint got no daddy, bitch," a voice yelled back.

"My momma says my daddy's in prison. Bobby aint my daddy!" I shot back sharply, doing my best to sound confident in the face of the unrelenting attacks.

"He aint yo daddy? We know he aint yo daddy. We all know him, and he aint got no white kids. Your momma just one a his bitches he stay wit. Ya'll don't even belong here, ya honkey bitches!"

An especially sweaty boy standing right in front of me added.

The largest boy stepped forward, "I don't give a shit where yo daddy is. He aint here and we gonna kick yo ass," and he punched me in the head. My legs gave out from the sudden pain and I fell head first to the ground.

As I drew my limp body into a familiar fetal position, the beating began and the chanting resumed.

BoBos, they make ya feet feel fine,

BoBos, cost a dollar ninety-nine,

BoBos, even the welfare will provide!

Kicks and punches landed on my back and legs. My body scraped against the ground, and I felt asphalt tearing into my skin. Someone was pressing my feet into the hard ground and I could feel the sneakers ripping apart. Realizing my shoes were being destroyed, I knew this beating would be nothing compared to the one I would get when I got home. Suddenly I started to cry.

The crowd heard my sobs and beat me harder. I could feel their heavy breathing as they crouched down to punch me. Their sweat dripped onto my face and mixed with my tears.

My right side ached with road rash as I lay on the scorching hot ground. Immobilized beneath the monkey bars, the kicks and punches suddenly became less intense and less frequent. The chanting and laughing had stopped, and I heard yells and screams that weren't my own. The beating stopped. I moved my arms from my head and opened one eye. I could see Matthew wildly swinging a large piece of wood. He was hitting the boys as he climbed inside the monkey bars. Bleeding and burning, I watched as he slammed the splintered wood with as much force as he could into the heads of each of the boys who had not run away. When the crowd scattered and we were left alone beneath the hot bars, Matthew reached down and jerked me from the ground,

not in tenderness but embarrassment. I stood up the best I could.

He looked down at me, my head hanging but my eyes glued to him. He spoke without a hint of irony, "You know you gonna be in trouble?"

I rubbed my arms trying to shake off the beating. "They won't know if you don't tell," I said sheepishly.

"Know? Everyone knows. How do you think I got over here? I was playing over there," he pointed into the distance but I knew where he meant, "and some kids started yelling about a fight and I grabbed a piece of wood to come join the fight. I didn't know it was you getting beat up. Why did you let all those guys hit you? Why didn't you go home?" He was angry with me, and he reached back like he was going to smack me with the piece of wood he still carried, but instead he threw the wood behind us and walked me home in silence. Battered and bruised and steadying myself for what was to come, I walked

home slowly, soaking in what I could of the sun as we walked between the buildings. I knew it would be a long time before I was let out of the house again.

When we reached the open doorway, Matthew did hit me. We stood side by side in the musky hall, as I waited for him to go up the stairs first. He smacked me hard on the back of the head and snarled, "What are you waiting for? Get up there. You already know what's gonna happen." His words hurt more than his hand. He had learned so much from Bobby. Matthew idolized Bobby as if he was his own father, and Bobby treated him with the same admiration. Matthew was a little version of Bobby.

Stumbling forward, I grabbed the railing and pulled myself up onto the stairs. Taking each step carefully, as though I might fall down, I only moved along because Matthew was behind me, pushing me up the stairs. I was sore, bleeding, and panicked from what awaited. I didn't know if

Bobby was there, but I knew he'd be there eventually. We got to the landing between the second and third floors faster than I wanted. I froze in place. Matthew pushed me to move on, and I fell forward. I threw my hands out in front of me to break my fall but still banged my chin on the step.

"Go on," he sounded tired and unconcerned.

I remained on the ground as long as he'd let me. He yanked me from the ground again, and I walked up the last few steps to the door. Again I froze in place; again Matthew prodded me forward by reaching over me and turning the knob. The door swung open, and I thought I was safe until the door bounced shut almost immediately. Matthew knocked on the door, and a voice boomed from the other side.

"Who da hell is it?"

"It's me dad. And Greg."

There was some noise from behind the door before it opened wide. I was still frozen in front of the door when it swung open.

"Get da fuck in here you two." He reached his arm out and pulled Matthew into the apartment. Bobby stared down at me and growled, "Get in here!"

I shuffled into the apartment. I saw Debbie sitting with her back to the door. Bobby turned to Matthew, "What happened to him?"

"Some kids were beating him up on the playground when I got there," Matthew began but he was interrupted.

"I know dat. I saw dat from the street. I wanna know what happened to the gotdamn shoes."

Matthew began again and was interrupted again. Bobby waved him away and Matthew went to the couch, threw himself down and stared at the television.

"Boy, what happen ta yo damn shoes?"

"I, I was, I was outside on the playground and some kids came and started hitting me and stepped on my shoes." I couldn't look at him as I spoke, and I tried to look at the ground without looking at my shoes. My new shoes were ripped, dirty and unsalvageable. Distracted by my shoes, I had not noticed Debbie's crying until she turned around to face us. Her makeup was running down her face in a familiar tear-stained pattern. Her voice was choked through her tears.

"Baby, I'm sorry about the money. I didn't know. I swear it was only ten dollars." At the sound of Debbie's voice, I stood up straight and turned toward her. She was shaking as she sat in the thin kitchen chair.

"Why you gonn take my money for dis mufucka anyway? I told you I don' want you spendin' my money on dis asshole. An' what dis boy doin out the gotdamn house anyway? I told you 'bout dat," he cocked his head toward me, "and *you* know better." With the final word Bobby

unbuckled his belt and pulled it free from his pants. He reached forward with his free hand and grabbed my hair. He stepped toward Debbie, pulling me with him. Turning to look at me he began again, the thick leather belt dangling from his right hand.

"You gon' go outside an tear up dem new shoes *I* bought fa ya?" He held me at arms length away with my hair firmly in his hand. His large right arm whipped back then forth and the belt came down wrapping across Debbie's back. Her whimper became a shriek.

"Now you care bitch? Now you think dis mufucka needs some shoes? You like dat? You buy dis bastard shoes wit my gotdamn money and he goes an' gets dem all torn up before I get home," his voice was rising as he whipped the belt back and forth across Debbie's back again. She drew her legs up into the chair and cradled her head between her knees. Her back began to swell

beneath her thin blouse when the belt came down again.

"I'm su, su, sorry baby. I'll get it back." Bobby pulled the belt back

I stood there at the end of Bobby's arm waiting for the beating to begin. Bobby faced me and smiled.

"So ya wanna fight? Ya like ta fight, ya little faggot? I taught ya all about it, yer brother know how ta fight. Shit, he had ta come an' get yer ass. I saw dat from da window." He shook me by my hair and threw me at my mother. I skidded across the linoleum floor, knocked my head against the seat of the chair and fell at Debbie's feet.

"You two little bitches belong together." Bobby snarled in disgust.

"Matt, who taught you ta fight?" Bobby asked the air as he stared at the ceiling. I reached up from the floor and grabbed Debbie's shins for comfort.

"You did daddy," Matthew sang from the living room.

Separated by a couch, the living room and the kitchen were one large room at the front of the apartment. I could see Matthew sitting on the couch from my spot on the kitchen floor. I stared at the back of his head as he watched "The Six Million Dollar Man" on the TV that sat against the far wall.

"Now boy, if I taught him ta fight why didn't you learn nuthin'?" He didn't wait for me to answer. He folded the belt in half and held it with both hands. Pushing the ends together, he pulled the looped belt taut ferociously. Debbie and I leapt at the terrifying snap of the leather.

"I'ma toughen you up boy, I'ma make you a man like yo brotha ova' ere." He knocked his head to the right indicating Matthew reclining on the couch without a care.

Hatred welled up inside me as I cowered at my mother's feet while she cried. My hatred grew as Bobby prowled around the kitchen and living room. My hatred for Bobby spawned from

beating Debbie and me while treating Matthew like a king, my hatred for Matthew spawned from his worship of Bobby, and my hatred for Debbie spawned from her failing to protect me. I stared up at Debbie and gripped her legs tighter.

"Get up," Bobby ordered from across the room. He was standing next to Matthew with a menacing look. I stayed in my spot at Debbie's feet, too afraid to move.

"I said get up boy and I aint bullshittin' Get up! We gonna make a man outta you right now."

I pulled myself up Debbie's shins and got to my feet. My ripped sneakers made me unstable as I stood. I balanced myself by leaning on her still-shivering body.

Debbie wrapped her arms around me and held me to her.

"Please don't do this. I'll make the money back tonight. I promise," she pleaded.

"Dis aint about no money. Dis about that bitch gettin his ass kicked every time he leaves this

gotdamn house. Gimme dat boy." Debbie
relinquished her grip and put her hands on my
shoulders, gently pushing me forward.

Stumbling toward Bobby as he moved to the
center of the wide room, I recognized the rage on
his face.

"Make a fist, boy. Show me your fists. We gonna
teach you ta fight." He put his hands up and
moved his feet into a fighting stance.

I stood before him, put my hands up and
mimicked his stance.

"Hit me, hit me now boy."

I stood motionless with my fists balled loosely in
front of me.

"HIT ME BOY!" he screamed loosing his
patience.

I swung my arm toward him, and he slapped it
away with his strong, callused hand. I spun
around with the force of his slap. Losing my
balance in my torn shoes, I fell to the ground.

Looking down at me, Bobby began to laugh as he said, "Boy, you aint shit and you aint ever gonna be shit. Now get up!"

Setting my hands on the floor behind me, I pushed myself up. I presented myself to Bobby with my hands to my side. His punch landed on my forehead, knocking me immediately back to the floor.

"I'm tellin' you boy, you aint ever gonn' be shit. You aint gonn' get outta here tonight if you don't fight back. Come on boy, get up." He walked a few steps into the kitchen, went to the refrigerator and got a beer, as I tried to lift myself from the ground.

"Boy, yo problem is you can't make no fist. Let me show you," he approached me slowly while taking a long pull from his beer. He put the beer on the stove and stood in front of me. His hands were cold and damp from the beer when he grabbed my hands and manipulated my fingers. He pushed my thumb into my palm and wrapped

my fingers around it. I was confused and my fingers were uncomfortable by the fist he had made.

"Bobby, don't. He's gonna get hurt, he's gonna break his hand," Debbie's voice was back to normal as she sat at the table smoking a cigarette. Her words and inaction ravaged my heart. She never moved from her chair to defend herself or me.

"Bitch, dis boy need to know how ta fight if he gonna live tonight. Shut up an' let him learn or you gonna be nex'." She was dismissed without a look.

"Boy, dis what you gon' do. Get yo ass out in'at hallway an' you gone use dis fist to knock on da door. When I can hear you, I'll let you in." He wrapped his hand over my tiny fist and squeezed. My thumb was uncomfortable and I knew something was wrong.

Debbie protested while Bobby pushed me out into the hall, "He's gonna break his thumb hitting

the door the way you want him to. He'll break his thumb." She was crying again, her knees up and her arm extended with the cigarette smoldering, sending a veil of smoke before her tear-soaked face.

"Baby, you need to shut up. You done wasted my money on dis bastard, you caint work tonight, and now dis little bitch is gonna learn to be a man. If he don't, I'ma kill both a ya. Now shut da hell up. Look he aint gonna break no thumb." He wrapped his hand into the same fist he had made out of my hand and punched her in the side of the head knocking her out of the chair.

"See bitch," he laughed as he raised his out stretched hand in the air, "my thumb aint broke." Without another look Bobby stepped toward me and guided me to the door. He pulled it open and shoved me into the dark hall.

"Boy, you keep knockin' like I showed you. When I can hear you I'll let you in and we'll try again. But I aint fightin no little bitch that can't make no

fist." The door slammed in my face and I was standing alone in the near darkness.

I stood for a moment, my fist still formed into Bobby's fist. I pounded on the door with the bottom of my fist, but with the first hit my hand stung, and pain shot through my body. I cradled my fist in my other hand.

Through the door I heard Bobby yell, "I don't hear nothin boy, you better be knockin' louder." Facing that door I harnessed all the anger I felt and I heard Bobby's words in my head playing over and over, "Boy, you aint shit and you aint ever gonna be shit". I promised myself at that moment that no matter what happened, if I lived to make it away from Bobby I *would* be something and I would not ever be like these people, not Bobby or Debbie.

Unwrapping my fingers from Bobby's fist, I formed my hands into normal fists and pounded on the door with all of my energy. Doors opened around me, and as I swung my head and arms

wildly, I caught glimpses of curious eyes peeking out of the slightest cracks of chained doors. The neighbors never said a word, as I continued lashing out at the door. Finally exhausted, I threw my body against the door. Pressed against the door, I couldn't hear any sounds other than the TV from inside the apartment.

The stale air of the hallway burned my nostrils, but my mouth was too dry to breathe through. My chest heaved as I regained my will. I backed away from the door and sucked in a last deep breath before I began pounding on the door again. Sweat ran down my face, matting my curly hair to my forehead and stinging the cuts on my face. I punched the door with all of my strength, trying to get Bobby's attention, trying to get Bobby's respect. My mind trained on the door, I did not notice the man coming up the stairs behind me until he was almost next to me.

A big hand reached out from the darkness and shook my head, "Damn boy, you been playin'

outside all day? You all sweatin' and dirty as hell," his voice was kind and joyful, his big grin framed his gleaming teeth in the darkness. I didn't respond. He took his now wet hand from my head and wiped it on his pants then reached up and drummed on the door with ease but the noise echoed through the stairwell.

I heard his voice as the door swung open carelessly, "*That's* what I'm talking about boy" and Bobby's face beamed down at me for an instant. Then he noticed the man standing to my left, and I was inconsequential.

"Yo brother, ya got that play?" the smiling man asked in a hopeful tone.

"Yeah man, come on in," Bobby's voice was welcoming and his face still smiled, but he was no longer looking at me.

The man had come to score, and that meant money, and that made Bobby happier than anything else. The door was wide open as Bobby waved the man inside. The smell of marijuana

wafted into the hall from the smoke-filled room. The smiling man put his large palms on my sweaty back and pushed me in before him. "Come on lil' brotha," he sang, and we entered the apartment together.

Matthew was still on the couch watching TV, his long blonde hair draped over the top of the couch. Debbie was not in sight. Bobby went to the refrigerator and got a beer and picked up a joint that was already burning. He sat down at the kitchen table with his friend, and for now I was forgotten.

I walked the few steps back to the bathroom, and there I saw Debbie washing her face. We shared a quick glance, her lips parted as if to speak, but I walked on by. I entered the bedroom I shared with Matthew at the end of the short hall. Pulling off my shirt, I wiped it over my head and face. The shirt was wet with sweat and blood and covered in filth when I threw it on the floor. Looking down at my tattered new shoes, I knew

there would still be a price to pay and a promise I would have to keep.

Chapter Three
Fresh and Clean

"GET-OFF-OF-ME-NOW!" Garek screamed.

"Sir, we will get up when you have calmed down. As long as you're yelling and fighting me, I can't let you up." I spoke calmly and quietly.

"I'M TELLING MY MOTHER AND HER BOYFRIEND IS GONNA COME UP HERE AND KICK YOUR BUTT," he threatened.

Having given him the instruction he needed to be released, I remained silent as he screamed. I held him as gently as possible while restricting his movement. This was not the first time Garek and I had gone through this routine, but it was the first time he had hurt another student.

Garek was about 5'6" at 13 years old. He'd only been in my class for a few weeks and had been aggressive and disruptive since the first day. The other students warned him that he was making a mistake by acting out, but nothing seemed to keep him calm until he had tired himself out after

lashing out at me for several hours. Garek had never been confronted for his behavior and was used to getting his way through threats and intimidation. How I had not met him sooner than I did was beyond me.

Garek had been sitting at his desk, and without warning or provocation he started growling like an animal and threw a book at another student. Stunned by the impact, the assaulted student sat drooping in his chair while Garek approached. I moved hastily in his direction. He picked a book from a desk and threw it at me. I slapped the book toward the wall and moved more quickly. When I was in range he swung a fist at my head and started screaming obscenities. I spun him around using his own momentum and used the approved restraint techniques to control his movement and keep the other students safe.

As I cradled him in front of me, I spoke gently to assure him that he was safe but that he needed to calm down. Refusing to calm down, he slammed

his head back and forth, trying to hit me in the face. I moved my head in opposing motions to his, causing him more frustration. At the same time, my assistant removed the other students from the room and left Garek and me alone, except for a counselor from a local guidance agency who was on the phone with Garek's mother. The alternative behavior program contracted with a local agency to work within the behavior classrooms and in the community to bring support and services to the children and their families.

Garek's blood-curdling screams and the evacuation of my classroom had gotten the immediate attention of the office staff. An administrator opened the door slightly and stuck her head into the room. She waved and assessed the situation.

"Everything ok?" she asked calmly with a confident smile.

"Yes, ma'am."

"Does mom know?" she queried while nodding her head toward Garek, now lying prone on the floor.

Over Garek's manipulative cries of how I had punched or intentionally hurt him, I spoke with poise and composure, "Michelle called a minute ago and spoke with her; we're covered," came my cool reply.

The administrator, still peeking in the door, peered over at Michelle who was standing by the telephone on the wall. Michelle nodded, "Mom just asked us to call her back if he was going to be suspended, otherwise she said to do whatever we had to. She was very agreeable."

"Sounds good, let me know if you need anything," the administrator chimed as she pulled her head back and closed the door.

Garek's screams continued as he began to kick his legs up, trying to kick me in the head. His too large sandals flipped off his feet, and one made contact with my face. The odor was crushing to

my senses. Instantly I realized I'd smelled that smell before.

The room was empty except for Michelle, so I took an unprecedented chance. I eased my hands from Garek and stood up. As expected, Garek quit his tantrum and looked at me quizzically.

I walked to the back of the room and grabbed a chair and placed it in front of the sink in the back of the room. Opening the under-sink cabinet I grabbed a small hand towel.

"Sir, come on over there and have a seat please," I instructed as I patted the seat.

He stood up apprehensively, made his way to the chair without a word and sat down. He stared at me strangely.

"Thank you Sir. Now if you'd please slide those feet on up here."

He put his feet into the sink as I asked and I turned the water on to let it run until it was warm. Grabbing the bar of soap that sat by the

sink's edge I lathered up and pulled Garek's feet into the water's stream.

"So what'd you do last night?" I asked as if this occurrence was commonplace.

"I watched this cool movie that my mom rented about this killer who tricks people into killing themselves. Have you seen it?"

"Yes Sir, but you know the rule, no discussion of rated R movies in school." I smiled at him, and he returned the gesture.

"You asked."

"Ok, then what'd you do?"

"I made some spaghetti and played video games on my mom's boyfriend's PlayStation II. He left it at our house so I can play it." He was eager to talk and steadily becoming more animated. "I fell asleep playing God of War. Have you played that? It's awesome." His grin broadened.

"No Sir, but I've seen it played. But hold up, your mom lets you play that? That's a pretty mature game, not that you're not mature but you know

what I mean." I tried to sound reassuring without him noticing my quest for information.

"Oh, my mom went out right after I got home from school so she doesn't know I was playing it."

"But you said you fell asleep playing it. Didn't she notice when she came home?" I pried as I scrubbed his feet and ankles, then, pulling him forward washed his legs up to his knees. He never mentioned it or even looked into the sink but tugged his cargo shorts so they wouldn't get wet.

"She didn't come home until after I got up for school this morning and she went right to her room. I put the game back so no one would know I was playing it." He went on talking as I looked over to Michelle who was looking at me in amazement and wonder. I caught her eye; her expression changed, and we looked at each other knowingly. I rinsed Garek's feet and leg and handed him the towel.

"How big are these things, a size 9?" I asked as I held up one of his feet.

"10, my mom says I have my dad's feet," again he rambled on as he dried his feet. He didn't notice as I walked away.

"Will you go up to WalMart and grab a pair of size 10 sandals?" I asked Michelle.

"Heck yeah, I'll get Renee and we'll just go shopping, he's about my son's size I think we'll just grab some clothes while we're there," she said as the wheels began spinning in her mind. She smiled, concerned and uneasy as she walked away.

"Hey," I whispered after her, "get some shampoo too. Thanks." I sidled back over to Garek who was standing barefoot with the towel in his hand. He made a move toward his shoes.

"Garek, come on over here and have a seat. You can let your feet dry before sliding your sandals back on."

He moved in my direction and took a seat at the table facing me.

I broke into conversation before he could say a word, "When my brother and I were in foster care, we didn't get a lot of positive attention. There wasn't a whole lot of supervision so we didn't take very good care of ourselves. One day my brother took his shoes off and ran around the house singing at the top of his voice, 'Smell my feet - what an awesome treat,' over and over as he went speeding around the house. Everywhere he went this terrible smell lingered. It really smelled like something had died and he had put it in his shoes and walked around with it for a week. But this is also the same person who wouldn't brush his teeth in the morning, but instead would smoke a cigarette and think that it made his breath smell better. My point is that after that experience it's pretty easy for me to recognize when someone needs some personal care attention." I spoke with levity, trying not to be patronizing.

"Wait, why were you in foster care?" he asked.

"My biological mother went to prison, and my biological father was already in prison, so the state put me into foster care, and I stayed there for a long time, going from home to home."

"What happened to your parents?"

"They're dead now. They both died a few years ago."

"What happened to your brother?"

"He's in prison."

"What'd he do?"

"That's not something I'm willing to talk about."

"Was it bad?"

"Yes Sir, but it doesn't involve me, so it's not my place to talk about it."

"Have you ever been to prison Sir?" he asked nervously.

"Yes Sir," I said, pausing to let the answer sink in. His face became more intense and I continued, "to visit my brother and my biological mother."

He smiled, "Sir, that wasn't funny. I thought you were serious."

"I was serious, I've been in several prisons to visit people, but no Sir I've never been incarcerated. How about you? You ever been to prison?" I joked.

With a chuckle and a smile he answered, "No Sir."

We talked for close to an hour, as I stalled until Michelle and Renee could come back with his new shoes, so as not to make a big deal of it in front of the other kids who I knew were in the library. The librarian and I were friendly as we shared an immense love of books and respect for the library as a sacred place. She allowed me to use the library as a sanctuary when I had to clear the room for one reason or another.

I pulled a copy of Kurt Baumann's <u>The Hungry One</u> from the bookshelf behind me and asked Garek to read it out loud. He was an excellent reader with a tremendous vocabulary. He read the book with the ease and timbre of a much older reader.

"What do you think?" I asked as he closed the book.

"Is this supposed to be me? Do you think I'm Rum Tum Tum? Am I the hungry one?" his questions rang with annoyance but I was expecting his reaction.

"What if I'm the hungry one?" I pondered with him.

"Then I'm in trouble," he said, his smile returning.

"When I was your age, fairy tales were very important to me because somehow, some way, the kids and the mothers always seemed to work it out - one way or another. My life was always so far from a fairy tale, and I always felt so alone that I clung to these stories for hope. Do you ever feel like that?"

"Sometimes," he paused, "but it's more about my dad. I don't see him much and I wonder if he misses me like I miss him." His smile faded, but he maintained his eye contact.

"I know how you feel. I never really knew my dad, and I used to wonder the same thing." He kept talking about his dad until tears soaked his face. He wiped his face on his dirty sleeve several times but never stopped his endearing speech about his absent father. I sat and listened without taking my eyes from his. He needed to talk, and I needed to listen if we were going to get anywhere. He was giving me the details about swimming with his father in the pool beneath a waterfall when Michelle and Renee walked in loudly, their arms full of bags. He noticed them immediately. I spoke before he had a chance.

"Hey man, I had them get you some new sandals. Hope that's cool." I said with some hesitation.

"Yeah, I mean, yes Sir. I've been wearing my mom's boyfriend's sandals. He said he doesn't need them anymore." His smile stretched across his face, as the ladies approached with the bags.

"Look what we got," Renee sang, placing her bags at Garek's feet.

"We went a little crazy, but you haven't spent any money all year, so we spent it for you," Michelle said to me while looking at Garek, "This is all for you. If any of it doesn't fit, your mom can return it, or we'll do it. We don't mind." She put her bags next to the others.

"Thanks. Can I try them on now?" he asked while digging through the bags, pulling out an assortment of clothes and shoes.

"Go ahead Sir; it's all yours." I replied contentedly.

He went to the restroom with a bag of clothes he had chosen from his new wardrobe and came back looking like a showroom model, tags dangling from his outstretched limbs.

"You look great. Do you like it?"

"Yes Sir," he beamed.

"What do ya say we get those tags off of you, pack up the rest of this stuff and get the rest of the class so we can get on with our day?" I instructed more than asked.

"Sure, I mean, yes Sir."

Garek packed his treasures as I spoke with the ladies, quickly summarizing all that had happened since they'd been gone. When he was done, Garek stood before us awkwardly.

"I'm ready," is all he said.

"Cool, let's get out of here and find everyone else. Ladies, we shall return."

We left the classroom and headed toward the library.

"Mr. Love?"

"Yes Sir?"

"I'm sorry."

"No need to apologize to me. You didn't hit me with a book."

We moved along in resumed silence. When we entered the library, Garek found the boy he had hit and walked toward him. I heard his sincere apology. They shook hands and wandered together through the library. Thanking the librarian and my assistant for their patience, I

signaled for my boys to line up. They did so quickly and silently. I led my line with pride as we made our way back to class.

Chapter Four
Birthday Present

My body welled with fear and anticipation as I stood in the middle of the room staring at the door waiting for it to open. Today I turned five. The day had gone on as any other day. Except for the moment I was sent to my room there was no mention of my birthday. I was long past tired and I was ready for bed. I had been shut up in my bedroom for hours since my dinner of cold rice and beans after which Bobby had told me to go stand in my room and wait. I knew what was coming. Every year it was the same. Matthew and Bobby sparring in the living room as I sat eating at the table alone. I pretended not to see Bobby coaching and encouraging his favorite son to do his job while Debbie sat on the couch laughing. When I had finished eating and washing the dishes I climbed down from the milk crates stacked in front of the sink and Bobby seemed to notice me for the first time.

"Quit makin' so much damn noise mufucka! What the hell's yo problem? When you done get yo ass to yo room and wait on yo brother. We be in there in a minute with yo birthday present." He smiled at Matthew and rumpled his silky blonde hair with his enormous black hand. The contrast was overwhelming. Bobby loved Matthew and his love was reciprocated without question. I could do nothing right and could never win favor. I only existed to Bobby to keep Debbie in line. He hurt me to hurt her.

Standing there in our room I wanted to fall over asleep just as the door burst open. Seeing Matthew's face smiling up at Bobby aroused an unfamiliar feeling inside me. Suddenly I was not afraid. Suddenly I was filled with the rage of years of abuse and neglect. I wanted what Matthew had with Bobby. I wanted the love, the attention, and the carefree life.

"Get in there and kick his ass," Bobby encouraged as he brushed Matthew into the

bedroom. Matthew looked at me and sneered. I was already in the center of the room, the bed in front of me just left of the door, the closet on my right, a scatter of broken toys behind me. I had memorized the room as I stood there, preparing, ready, waiting. For the last two years, Matthew and I had fought as brutally as two young boys could. Each year I was left bleeding and semi-conscious on the floor. Bobby would burst into the room and raise his favorite son into his arms and abandon me in the darkness of the bedroom. This was my birthday present.

Matthew and I were the same age for one day. Each year on my birthday Bobby would toss Matthew and I into our bedroom and warn us that only one of us was allowed to emerge. The other was to be beaten until he could not get up. Each year I lost. Each year Matthew was rewarded. I lost because I was not used to fighting back. I was accustomed to Bobby's daily beatings.

Any sign of defense only brought a more aggressive beating.

This was my fifth birthday, November 10th, 1978. As I stood facing my brother he was no less than six inches taller than me. Lean and strong in contrast to my cherubic soft form, he had been nurtured by Bobby to be a fighter and a thief. He roared toward me to earn yet another victory. As he lunged forward I stepped out of his way and he stumbled over some of the toys on the floor behind me. With his face down on the floor I took my chance and jumped on him and pounded my tiny fists into every area of his back and head that I could reach. He squirmed and attempted to roll over. I lost my balance and fell forward covering his body with my own. Our heads collided before Matthew's head hit the floor. I sat up, higher now on his back and grabbed his hair. In a wild frenzy I smashed his face into the hard concrete floor. My knees pinned on his back he could not roll over and I could not stop myself from smashing

his face over and over again. My rage had taken over and I was lost in the new feeling of triumph.

"Ge'off, ge'off," I heard Matthew yelp. I ignored his pleas for release but allowed him to roll over. His face was red and beginning to bruise. His forehead and mouth were streaming blood. I balled my fists together and pounded them down onto his sculptured face like a hammer. His head bounced a last time before he spit blood onto my shirt. My energy was gone but I brought my fists down in a flurry of connecting blows to each side of his face. I had never fought so much before and soon I had no energy to continue the combat. I stood up and kicked him in his ribs. He rolled over to avoid another kick but I kicked him in the back. A tooth fell out of his mouth in a pool of blood as he began to scream. His scream was loud and strangled with blood. I heard the door open behind me then quickly slam shut. Bobby said something I could not hear through the door but I could hear him laughing.

Reinvigorated by Bobby's laughter, I jumped back on Matthew and pounded my tiny soft fists at any surface of his body I could reach. His blood excited and disgusted me at the same time. I knew if I left Matthew conscious he would get up and pounce on me before I left the room. Matthew wasn't moving. He had stopped struggling and screaming. I could feel him breathing beneath me but I could not stop my attack. I had been attacked so many times by Bobby, Debbie, Matthew, and all of the neighborhood kids and all of those beatings produced an anger I had never known until I sat on top of Matthew and watched the blood pour from his mouth. His face was swollen to resemble my own. Bobby's words of encouragement to Matthew rang in my head. I knew I had won and it felt good. For the first time I felt good and *I* wanted to be rewarded.

I was sweating as I stood up and looked down at my brother prone and motionless on the floor. I

felt that I had finally become the son Bobby had always wanted, another fighter, and another strong protégé, to be paraded about in front of the endless parties of friends as he did with Matthew. I kicked Matthew one last time before I walked backward to the door making sure he was not getting up. He did not move as I clicked the light off and opened the door and emerged victoriously clomping breathlessly into the short hall toward the living room.

"Damn boy, you good. That was fast. Come on and have a seat," Bobby said without turning away from the television. I stumbled into the living room and presented myself before Bobby and Debbie, my clothes covered in Matthew's blood. Bobby's hand came up and slapped the side of my face before I ever noticed his hand move.

"What the fuck you doin' out here boy?" Bobby bellowed.

"Where tha fuck's yo brotha?" he screamed as I tried to raise myself from the floor quickly but the kick came and knocked me on my back, as he yelled, "Don't get all that gotdamn blood on my floor, get the fuck up boy. What the fuck you doin out that room?"

We got up at the same time. Bobby raised himself from the couch as I scurried across the living room floor trying to avoid being hit. Bobby moved quickly toward the bedroom while yelling back that I had better not have hurt his son. Debbie moved from the couch and smiled at me without saying a word. I scuttled back away from her but she caught me easily and drew me up into her arms.

"I love you baby, I'm so sorry. Happy birthday. I'll get you a present soon, I promise." She smiled slightly and with her face close to mine she began to cry and repeated, "I'm sorry." I knew there would be no present.

Before I could say a word, Bobby exploded into the room holding Matthew's limp body.

"Get a gotdamn washrag. Get this boy cleaned up. What tha fuck you think you doin' hittin' your gotdamn brother like this? I'ma kick yo ass!" He gently placed Matthew on the couch as Debbie scampered to the adjoining kitchen, returning quickly with a wet rag and began dabbing Matthew's face. The same rage welled up inside me as Matthew's limp body was so tenderly laid out on the couch. On this same night each year previously I had been left alone in the dark to wake up in the morning covered in blood and bruises which I had to clean myself while the rest of the family celebrated Matthew's birthday.

When he saw Debbie dutifully cleaning Matthew, Bobby unbuckled his belt and whipped it out of his pants. The familiar crack brought me to attention across the small living room. I stood by the television where Debbie had left me and now

I realized I was cornered. The belt swung down and slashed me across the face. I fell to my knees and covered my face with my hands. The belt continued to rain down again and again until blood from my hands streamed into my eyes and mouth. Semiconscious, I bled out onto the floor. Bobby reached down and lifted me by one arm and dragged me to the couch where Matthew was recovering and seemed to be gaining consciousness. Debbie had his mouth open and was applying an ice-filled baggie to the space in his mouth where his tooth had been.

"So you big now? You gonna beat yo brother like you got something? Show me what da fuck you got. Come and gimme some of that, big man!" Bobby was yelling at the top of his voice.

Debbie looked up from tending Matthew, "Baby you told them to fi-". Before the word was out her mouth, Bobby's mighty arm had slung the belt down across her back. "Bitch, this don't concern

you." Bobby wheeled around and slashed my face with an up-handed whip of his belt.

"You like that shit, make you feel big don't it?" Blood poured onto the floor though it went unnoticed in Bobby's fury. My hair was sticking to my eyes and forehead. I couldn't see clearly but I saw Matthew moving on the couch. Bobby saw him too. His attention turned quickly as if I had never been there.

"How you doin boy?" Bobby spoke gently as his rage transformed into concern, though he still clutched the belt firmly in his hand.

"Awight," replied Matthew, now sitting up on the couch. "My mouf 'urts," he mumbled shakily.

"What the fuck you doin lettin' dis asshole hit you like this? Yo face all red and ya got a toof knocked out. What the fuck is this boy? I taught you better than this. Gonna let this asshole kick yo ass?"

Matthew tried to explain but his voice only made Bobby laugh and it was impossible to hear what Matthew was saying.

"Get me a beer bitch, and get some for the boys too. Shit I guess they earned that shit this time." He was speaking to Debbie but he spun around and stared at me as if seeing me for the first time since bringing Matthew out of the bedroom.

"SO, you a badass now?" Bobby barked with a half-smile.

I stood frozen having not been given permission to speak. For a brief moment I felt a spark of pride through the stinging pain tearing through my body. Debbie handed me a bottle of beer. The cold glass felt good against my swollen hands. I switched the bottle from hand to hand as I wiped the blood from my hands onto my pants so I could hold the beer. I took a drink and felt the liquid sting the open cuts in my mouth.

"Well boy, I'm talking to you, answer me."

"No. I was doing what you told me to do. I didn't mean to hurt him."

"BULLSHIT!" his voice boomed inside the tiny apartment and the beer slipped from my hands as I shook. I caught the bottle as it slid down my legs. Bobby approached and bent down, putting his face in mine.

"When you hit someone you hit them to hurt them. You always mean to hurt someone you hit, that's why you hit them. That's why you always lose when those boys out there kick yo ass and that's why you lose when yo brother kicks yo ass. You're too much uva pussy to hit anyone." He took a long pull from his beer and reached for the joint Debbie was smoking. She handed it to him and he took a drag. Then he handed the joint to me.

"I guess you not a pussy tonight now are ya? Ya little prick." He turned again to Matthew as I grabbed the burning joint from his giant fingertips.

I set my bottle on the floor and held the joint in my lips. After my hands were dry and free of blood, I balanced the joint in my mouth and took a quick drag and then another. The smoke burned but it was familiar and pleasant. I coughed a little as I reached for my beer. I walked to the couch and handed the joint to Debbie. She looked at me with pride as she reached out her thin fragile fingers. Her dirty fingernails caressed the back of my hand and a chill ran through my body. I was so unaccustomed to my mother's delicate touch.

"Give that shit back, he earned it," Bobby commanded. Debbie's trance-like gaze was broken and she looked up at Bobby from the couch. She put her feet on the floor and leaned forward to hand the joint back to me. I took the burning joint from her outstretched fingers and raised it to my lips without looking at her again. Before I could taste the warming smoke Bobby's

hand had smacked the side of my head rushing
me away from the living room.

"Now get the fuck outta here, I can't stand
lookin' at you." Bobby snarled without looking at
me. His attention fully trained on Matthew. I was
too stunned to move and Bobby did not notice
that I was still in the room.

"Drink up boy, you feel better in a minute."
Bobby was cooing at Matthew. He tilted
Matthew's beer making foam run down his chin.

"My mouf 'urts," Matthew said again.

"Boy, I don't wanna hear that shit outch yo mouf
ever again. I don't care how bad you beat you
don't ever say you hurt. You hear me? Aint no
son a mines gonna be talking 'bout bein' hurt.
That some pussy ass shit and you aint no pussy
ass nigga like yo brother. Ya hear me boy?"
Matthew nodded. He brought the beer to his
mouth again.

Bobby slapped Matthew's leg and stared down
sternly, "You will not lose to that boy again, ya

hear me?" Without giving Matthew a chance to respond he moved his giant hand to Matthew's back and pushed him off of the couch.

"It's probably time for your birthday now, get ya'self another beer and get that joint from yo brother. Good night boy."

Bobby fell onto the couch as Matthew walked triumphantly to the kitchen. As he walked around the far side of the couch I limped off into our bedroom unnoticed, smoking as much of the joint as I could get down before having to hand it off to Matthew who I knew would not give it back.

Chapter Five
Shades of the Past

Standing on the chipped concrete steps in my teacher clothes, I knew I still looked more like a cop than a teacher, having often been mistaken for such, even in school. I knocked on the plexiglass storm door. The inner door was open, and I could see three adults, two men and a woman - all under 25 - sitting in various spots in the living room. When I knocked, two of them looked up at me for a second and looked away. One of them spoke to the young man sitting in the corner. He was busy counting a large stack of money, and there were several other stacks on the table in front of him. Next to the money, I could see what appeared to be bricks of marijuana, but I could not be sure. Directly in front of me (on the coffee table just inside the door) was a row of blunts: large marijuana cigarettes wrapped in a cigar shell.

The young woman closest to the door waved me in without a word.

"Hi, I'm Greg Love, Deondre's teacher. Is his mom at home?" I asked politely.

"You Deondre's teacher for real?" asked the woman who had waved me in, caressing her pregnant belly.

"Yes ma'am," I replied.

She smiled a wide, gapped-tooth grin, "My name Tamesha. I'm Deondre's sister. Momma aint home right now, but she be back in a minute if you wanna wait," she offered.

"That'd be great. Thanks a lot." I stood to the side of the door, waiting to be asked to sit or to be introduced to the other people in the room, but no one spoke. The young couple on the couch just stared at me through deeply stoned eyes. Trying not to look at the obvious mounds of marijuana on the kitchen table and the stacks of cash beside them, I looked around the small room. It was cluttered with baby toys,

newspapers, fast food bags, pictures and cheap paintings leaning against the walls. To my right sat a large projection television nearly as tall as myself. In front of it on the floor lay an old dissected VCR and a PlayStation. To my left, just inside the door, was a large glass aquarium in which lay a huge ball python. Lamps with bare light bulbs sat on TV trays, strewn around the room. The room and the surrounding rooms that I could easily survey were tidy but not clean.

The young man in the corner looked up from his counting. As he wrapped the stack of cash in his hand with a rubber band, he spoke at last: "You Deondre teacher?"

"Yes Sir, I'm Greg Love." I extended my hand to him as I stepped toward him. He leaned forward and shook my hand in several complicated, yet familiar, motions. His blank expression evolved into a half smile.

"Tony," he said squarely as a means of introduction. I recognized the name, and I knew I

was speaking with Deondre's older brother, the man of the house.

"What's up? We aint ever had no teacher come by here before." The young man sat back in his chair, staring me directly in the eyes.

"Deondre's been having some trouble in class and I was hoping to talk to his mom. . ." Before I could finish my sentence, Tony stood up and yelled for Deondre.

Deondre appeared sheepishly from an unlit hallway off the main room, his head held low.

"Good afternoon Sir." I greeted him cheerfully.

"What's this about you causing trouble in school?" Tony demanded.

"I don't know." He mumbled, his head still down.

"Boy you better answer my question right. What the hell you been doin' at school?"

Deondre stood still and silent.

Tony looked from Deondre to me. "What's he doin'?"

"There's quite a bit really. He's been very aggressive with other students, he's not doing his work, and several times he's tried attacking me. I've been calling but I couldn't get a hold of anyone; that's why I'm here." I explained in my most teacher-like fashion.

Tony considered my words and looked as if he was about to speak. Instead he erupted in a fury of violence, attacking his younger brother.

Deondre cowered under the abuse, as I instantly regretted speaking to Tony. Images of Bobby flashed through my head. Pain and anger swelled in my mind. It was not my place to intervene, and I tried to keep my irritation to myself.

Deondre was helpless on the ground, but Tony continued his tirade and his beating.

In too-familiar breathlessness, Tony stood and asked me if there was anything else Deondre was or was not doing.

I stood firm and answered with my common courtesy, "No Sir."

"Go get your homework and get it done, NOW!"
Tony commanded his brother. Less than half his
brother's size, Deondre stood up and moved back
through the darkness from which he had
appeared, and I heard a door close.

The two silent observers on the couch never
moved during the outburst. When Tony sat back
down, he offered me a seat.

"So you come ta student's houses all the time?"
Tony asked as if we had just been introduced.

"All the time actually. I'm sorry I didn't call first,
but I couldn't get through. Deondre's a good kid.
He's got a good heart. We just have to find it.
He's got a lot of anger that he's holding inside,
and right now he's acting it all out at school." I
repositioned myself in my chair and made myself
at home. It seemed I would be there a while.

"You come 'round this part o' town all the time
too?" Tamesha asked with a glazed stare.

"Yes I do. I've got friends all over this part of town," I replied and spun my finger in the air indicating the neighborhood.

"Like who?" Tony asked in a disbelieving tone. I rattled off a list of names he was sure to recognize. "I used to live on this side of town a few years ago before I was a teacher." The names had an obvious effect on Tony's disposition. He stood again and offered me some Kool-Aid. I thanked him as we drank our purple drink together.

The young man on the couch finally made a move, as Tony and I talked over our drinks. "You wanna get high man?" the young man without a name slurred.

"No, thanks man, I'm cool," I cocked my head and held my palm up like I was stopping traffic.

"I don't know when my mom's gonna get back. I'll tell her you came by if you got somewhere to be," Tony offered kindly.

"I have the time if you don't mind me hangin' out. I really want Deondre to know that I'm serious. It's really important to me that he understands that I care enough to spend the time," I said sternly.

"That's cool, man. We just chillin' anyway. What's your name?" Tony asked pleasantly.

"Greg Love," I smiled, unsurprised that he didn't recall my name.

The storm door creaked open, and a large middle-aged woman stepped into the room to a cheerful welcome. Almost in unison, all three of the residents called, "Hey momma."

"Whose Jeep is that in the," momma began, stopping short as she noticed me sitting in the corner across from Tony.

I stood up confidently and introduced myself. She was kind and welcoming.

"Have a seat honey; I'll be right with you." She turned to Tony and quietly asked him to move his stuff so she could sit down.

"Where's Dee?" she asked Tamesha.

"He in his room," she replied.

"Dee!" His mom called from the chair Tony had been sitting in.

Deondre appeared quickly, holding a book and some papers.

"Hey momma," he said uncomfortably.

"What's your teacher doing here honey?"

"I, I wa'n't doin' my work and…" his voice trailed off.

"And what honey, tell your momma, Dee." Her voice was reassuring and very kind. Her honest motherly concern broke through his front, and he looked at her, his face full of disgrace.

"I was wrestlin' in class and… I tried to hit Mr. Love, and he restrained me." His voice was soft and embarrassed.

"Is that true?" She asked me, sounding displeased. I wasn't sure if she was upset with her son or me.

"Yes ma'am, it is. Michelle and Renee tried to call to let you know, but they couldn't get a hold of you. They offered to come by earlier, but I told them I'd come by myself since we hadn't met yet." I was rationalizing, thinking I had to justify my presence and my actions.

She sat up and looked sadly at Deondre. "Dee you know better. Mr. Love, I'm sorry if he caused you any trouble. Dee, go get your books and come sit here at the table and finish up your homework." She sat back in her chair and took off her shoes.

We talked for a long time, as Deondre completed his homework sitting between us. She told me of her troubles, financial and medical. She opened up about Deondre's social and school history, information that wouldn't be found in any file. He'd had a less-than-easy life including witnessing his grandfather's death in a farming accident. His father was in and out of his life, and now his brother was his father figure and disciplinarian.

She never mentioned the drugs or the money that had been laid out before us when she had entered the room. The money I had seen was not part of her economic situation. I learned later that Tony's business was his own and his mother would not accept his money.

As I left with Deondre's homework in my hand, his mother welcomed me back anytime, saying her door was always open for me. I was pleased I had come and felt a new connection with Deondre. I drove home contemplating all that had happened. Thoughts of the beating kept Bobby weighing heavily on my mind.

Factoring in my newly acquired knowledge, I changed my approach to Deondre. I spent more time with him and concentrated on our relationship. The school days following my visit were quiet and peaceful. Deondre had been an impetus for disruption in the class, and his new attitude had a calming affect on the class. His schoolwork had improved along with his

behavior. For weeks this pattern continued. I visited his house frequently to provide positive updates and solidify the relationship between home and school.

Then came a gradual but noticeable decline, first in appearance, then schoolwork, and finally in behavior. I went immediately to Deondre's house after school on the day I had to restrain him. His mother was home, and she was not surprised by what I told her. She explained in more detail the extent of her financial circumstances: she was on the brink of being of being evicted, the water had been shut off a week earlier, and the electricity was due to be cut within the week. Her situation was too familiar. There were resources available to her, and I left promising that I would do what I could to find them for her. Her bills were extraordinarily high, and it would cost a couple of favors to pull off what I had in mind. In my car I called some friends, Michelle and Renee first. I

told them what needed to be done, and they said they would make some calls themselves.

The next day at school, I sent Michelle and Renee around town visiting churches and charities, making deals, and calling in favors. By the end of the day, arrangements had been made to meet nearly all of Deondre's family's expenses, including groceries. The one account we could not clear was a nearly $300 phone bill. None of us knew anyone with influence at the cell phone company. While home visits were easy enough for us to make, we all appreciated the true necessity of a phone, especially with children in the house. I took out my checkbook and wrote a check for the full amount. Michelle and Renee objected to my decision, but I wouldn't listen. With instructions for them to pay the bills, then visit the house to inform Deondre's mom that all her bills were paid (but not to tell her I paid anything) I waved the ladies away.

Deondre returned to school the next day clean and happy. He handed me a piece of paper he said was from his mother. It was a heart-wrenching thank you letter with prayers of thanks and praise. There was also an invitation to stop by the house. I passed the letter to the ladies and asked if they would make some follow up calls to everyone who had assisted us the day before to thank each of them in turn, from us and the family.

I drove to the house after school and was greeted this time with a deep embrace from Deondre's mom in the driveway. She pulled me inside and cleared a chair, so I could sit down. She sat across from me, as she had when we first met. Through her tears, she declared that God had sent me into her life, but I convinced her it was school and nothing else. Her faith would not let her accept my rationale. As we sat there, Deondre came in and plopped onto a chair at his mother's side.

I sat with them longer than I ever had. Deondre's mother and I traded personal stories until I had her laughing her glorious hearty laugh. It seemed like as good a time as any to propose an idea I'd had since I saw Tony's "fathering" techniques.

I started in, "Ma'am, my goal is to get Deondre out of the behavior program and back into his regular school. I've seen that he can do the work and he can control his behavior, he just needs the right motivation. He and I have been doing some great work at school and I'd like to see that continue."

"Me too. You're the first man teacher he's ever had that he seems to respect. He really likes you, you know?" She said with a smile.

"That's great. I know he doesn't have a lot to do on the weekends, and you have too much to do. I was hoping the three of us could make a contract that would motivate Deondre to work his way out of the program as well as give him an opportunity to earn some money."

She was hooked, "What do you have in mind? Anything that will help would be great. I'm out of ideas, and I really don't want him making too many friends in this neighborhood."

"We'll make a contract that says for every positive week Deondre has at school--working toward leaving the program--I will bring him to my house that Saturday. We'll work together in the yard or on the car, whatever needs to get done. I'll pay him $10 an hour and he can work as little or as much as he'd like. I'll pick him up and drop him off." The more I spoke the more she smiled. When I was done she looked at Deondre and asked, "What do you think Dee?"

"I'll do it. I can do that. Is it real money?" he asked through his smile.

Looking at him sternly I replied, "Yes Sir, it is. As long as it's real work." Then I turned my eyes to his mother who hadn't yet given her thoughts.

"I think it sounds great. He's always asking to go somewhere on the weekends, but Mr. Love, I just

don't have that kind of money. If you're willing to do it I support you 100 and 10 percent!" Her words were serious and sorrowful.

"Believe me, I don't have that kind of money either. But I work two jobs, and I'm willing to invest in this." I said frankly.

We spoke for nearly an hour, hammering out the details and making up a timeline for Deondre to earn his way back to his regular school. Sitting at the kitchen table, I wrote it up, we all agreed on the terms, and then each of us signed the contract. Shortly afterward, I left the house with a renewed sense of purpose.

School became calm again, and the days sailed smoothly by. Deondre kept our contract quiet, just as we'd agreed. For safety I made sure Michelle and Renee knew the entire agreement. They convinced me to inform the administration. This turned out to be a good idea. The principal called Deondre's house and confirmed the agreement. When she put the phone down she

looked across her desk. Her apprehension was obvious, but her confidence in me won out.

"If this works out I'll expect you to take all of the kids home, you realize that?" she joked.

Saturday came and I drove into Deondre's driveway. He was ready when I stepped up to the door.

"Good morning Sir. We're going to be working outside today. You may want to bring some clothes to change into after we're done if you want to still see that movie," I said to him as he opened the door.

He ran away back to his room and reappeared quickly with his bulging book bag. I stood in the living room and exchanged pleasantries with his mother who was sitting in her chair.

"You sure you wanna do this?" she was talking to me.

"Yes ma'am, he's earned it. We have to uphold our contract." I responded politely.

"If he gives you any trouble you have my permission to whip him," she warned, giving a smile to her son.

"I'd never hit a child, but thanks. I don't think there will be any problems." I shrugged off her comment and moved toward the door. I looked back to her, "You have my number in case of an emergency?" I asked, double-checking.

"Yes I do, right here in my phone," she said, happily waving goodbye with her pink phone in her hand.

After spending several hours working side-by-side in the yard, Deondre asked if we could stop. We packed up the tools, washed up, and I handed him two twenty-dollar bills. His face lit up with joy.

"This mines?" he cheered.

"What you should say is, 'Is this mine?' and yes Sir it is. But now whatever you want to do you have to pay for."

"Can we get some hot wings, please Sir?" he asked with uncertainty.

"Of course. Let's get out of here."

We drove to a local restaurant that specialized in chicken wings. Deondre was overwhelmed as if in a dream world. Wings were his favorite food and presented with so many choices he didn't know what to do. He stuck to what he knew and ordered a dozen as hot as he could get them. While we waited for our food he told me that this was his first real restaurant experience. He said the only restaurants he'd ever been to were the fast food places scattered around his neighborhood.

A few months went by this way. Deondre worked harder each week, and each week we had fun adventures that he'd never been able to do simply because of money. He got stronger and more self-confident as he worked to earn his own money. Then the trips after work became less frequent as Deondre started saving more and more of his

money. School became a pleasure for everyone as I spent my days teaching, not disciplining. When the semester ended Deondre had earned his way out of the program and back to his regular school. There was no long goodbye. Deondre and I did our best not to cry, I'm sure for different reasons. Our contract had expired and he was moving on. Not only would his commanding presence be missed in class, but also I had become used to our Saturday mornings together. He had grown so much since our time together began. He was a young man now, with confidence and discipline. When Deondre walked out of the building for he last time, I walked him to the door and shook his hand.

"I'm proud of you Sir," I spoke still trying not to cry.

The young man radiated confidence as he shook my hand firmly, "Me too."

Chapter Six

Kittens

There were unfamiliar sounds coming from our building that got louder as I got closer. Running in from school, I rounded the corner into the doorway to see one of the ladies from the first floor kneeling before a cardboard box beneath the stairs. In the pale darkness, I heard the small cries more clearly. They were loud, but I was mesmerized. Moving forward, I saw the woman cleaning a litter of kittens. She turned to me with a rag in her hands. The woman was caressing the kittens as gently as I'd ever seen anyone touch an animal. Animals in the Village were not prized or even common. There were a few stray dogs around that we often had to look out for when we were out at night, but not many people kept a pet of any kind.

The woman repositioned herself and smiled as I moved closer. I walked over to the cardboard box on the floor. I bent down and looked in

amazement at the newborn kittens. Without asking, I reached in and attempted to pick one up. As gently as she cleaned her new brood, the woman took my little hands and told me that I shouldn't pick them up just yet but I was welcome to sit and watch. I sat for a few moments longer then thanked the woman and made my way up the ominous stairwell.

Each night and day I looked forward to seeing the woman and her kittens. I stole precious minutes from each day after school to spend with the kind woman and her crying kittens. After a few days of watching at her side the woman handed me one of the tiny kittens. Nervously holding the kitten in my hands I knew I had never felt anything so soft. Transfixed, I sat down on the grimy floor. I held the kitten up and rubbed my face all over its furry body. I nuzzled my nose against it and breathed in the sour milk smell. Ambivalently, I handed the kitten back to the woman, thanked her, and ran quickly up the stairs. That night, I hid in my

room with my hands held to my face smelling the sour milk scent of the kitten, reliving the feel of the tiny animal.

Each day after school, the woman let me hold another kitten until I had had a chance to hold each one. Holding the kittens made my days pass more quickly and my nights more bearable, as I dissociated to my time with the kittens. Each day, as I continued to visit the woman, I saw the kittens growing. The time we spent together became more important each day as I found a kitten I favored most.

One afternoon there was a delicate knock on the door. Debbie opened the door and the cat lady from the first floor stood there with her hands close to her chest. I rushed to Debbie's side. The cat woman briefly explained that I had visited the kittens for weeks and that now they were old enough to feed themselves. She proffered Debbie my kitten. Standing at Debbie's knee I looked up at the woman and Debbie alternately. Few words

passed between them before the woman knelt down and handed me my favorite kitten.

Debbie closed the door and looked at me with pity in her eyes.

"I don't know what your father will say about this so you keep the cat in your room until I have a chance to talk to him." She reached down and touched the kitten with her fingertips.

"What are you gonna name it," she asked.

"I don't know." I was too ecstatic to think.

The kitten was purring in my ear when Debbie turned me around and shooed me toward my room. I moved slowly with the kitten held tight against my face, rubbing my head back and forth against its soft gray fur. During a forward swipe of my head the kitten nibbled my nose with its tiny teeth. I giggled and I pulled it away from my face. Wandering toward the bedroom I stared into the little sparkling eyes in front of me and felt true happiness.

Matthew was in the bedroom playing with our Spider-Man Colorforms on the floor. Until that kitten was placed in my hands the Colorforms were my favorite escape in my world of the tiny apartment. I placed the kitten on the floor and it stumbled around the cluttered floor. Matthew crept up beside me and together we followed the kitten around as it explored the room. The kitten meandered over every inch of the bedroom with Matthew and I following it on our hands and knees. Soon the three of us were meowing, purring, and scrambling around the room.

In my excitement I scuttled to the door to get Debbie's attention. I wanted her to see the kitten swatting a Webble Wobble around the floor. When the door opened the Webble Wobble came sailing past my feet and directly behind it came the kitten. The kitten ran faster in the wide-open space than I'd seen it move in the bedroom. Matthew and I chased it through the apartment

while the kitten chased the wobbling toy. I called for Debbie to watch.

As the kitten ran around her feet I witnessed uncharacteristic pleasure on her face. She got down onto the floor with her two sons and played with the kitten. She was more adept at catching the wily little creature than we were. Debbie lifted the kitten, rose up onto her knees and stroked its bushy coat gently before handing it back to me. I jostled it in my hands as it squirmed to break free. Without thinking I let the kitten loose on the floor and Matthew and I proceeded to chase it around the kitchen and living room area. Suddenly the door burst open and Bobby walked into the apartment.

His rage was instantaneous. Upon setting eyes on the kitten he began to unleash his anger upon Debbie who was caught off-guard by his sudden appearance.

"What you doin bringin' some filthy animal in my house? What da hell you think you doin'?" he screamed.

"I - didn't - do - baby," she sputtered through her sobs as Bobby pounded down on her, "it's - Greg's - kitten."

His fists stopped in mid-air and he sprang back. I was scurrying around the floor trying to catch and protect the kitten. Bobby lunged forward into the living room where I was huddled on the floor with the kitten safely in my arms. At his approach I pressed my face down into my folded arms covering the kitten. Bobby grabbed my exposed neck into his fist and pulled me from the floor. I held the crying kitten more tightly against my chest.

He dragged me to the window on the far wall next to the television. With his free hand he opened the window and jerked my head up to face him, still holding my neck with the other.

He plucked the kitten from my hands. Holding my beautiful kitten by the neck with his thumb and forefinger he dangled it before my face. "Don't you ever bring no shit like dis in my house again, ya hear me?" Before I could answer, he effortlessly flipped my kitten out the window like a Frisbee. He held my body up to the window and made me watch my kitten fall through the air and hit the ground.

He threw me away from the window and slammed it shut and pulled the shade down. In one step he was standing at my feet. He took another step forward and put a crushing foot onto my chest. I gasped for air and grabbed his foot. "Don't touch me wit' yo filthy hands," he hissed as he shook his leg loose from my grasp, kicking me in the face in the process.

"What da fuck you gon' do wit a damn cat in dis house? We got too many moufs ta feed already. I don't want no dirty animal in here with my baby girl." Bobby and Debbie had recently had a child

together, her name was Ruby and she was asleep in the next room. She was just under a year old and she was the most important person in the apartment as far as Bobby was concerned, even more important than Matthew.

He bent down putting his face where my kitten had been just moments before, "I don't want no filthy animal near my baby girl." He slapped me hard across the face.

"Do. You. Understand?" His emphatic speech was littered with spit.

I managed a whimpered, "Yes" before he slapped me again.

"I'ma make sure you understand boy!" He pulled me from the floor by my shirt and threw me against the wall. I shrank to the floor at impact.

"Get up. Get up. GET. UP!" He raged.

The force of the impact had made rising from the floor impossible. Bobby stormed across the small room and lifted me up again.

"You sonuvabitch, I said GET UP BOY!"

Raised to a standing position he held my limp body against the wall and slapped my face forcing my head into the wall with each backhanded blow. The smell of tobacco on his hands replaced the sweet smell of the kitten I cherished.

Debbie appeared behind Bobby and grabbed his waist pulling him toward her.

"Please baby, please let him go. He didn't know, he's sorry," she pleaded.

Though my ears rang I heard her words and I grew furious with her for letting Bobby believe I had brought the kitten into the house, for letting Bobby hurl my kitten out the window, for letting Bobby beat me. I was angry but helpless, pinned against the wall. Debbie's tugging on Bobby's waist was a fruitless effort. My beating continued and in a single motion he slapped me then Debbie, knocking her to the floor. Matthew as usual was nowhere in sight.

The beating continued until Bobby wore himself out. His heavy breathing was hot on my face. I

saw blood on his hands that was surely mine. He pulled his hand from my chest and let me fall to the floor. He walked away casually to the kitchen table. Through my swollen eyes I watched as he unloaded his pockets. Pulling a miniature manila envelope from his pocket he flipped the top and pressed it open. He dumped its contents onto the table. Debbie's formerly lifeless body was suddenly revived as she crawled to the table.

"Baby, let me get a bump, baby, please," she begged.

"Fuck you. You let your bastard kid bring that rat into my house an' now ya wanna bump off my shit?" he didn't take his eyes off of the powder that he smoothed out into a series of lines with the bottom edge of the miniature envelope.

There was more faint pleading and then shouting but the sounds became steadily more distant. Slumping further down the wall I drifted into unconsciousness.

I was kept home from school the next day since my face was swollen and there was no excuse to give to the school for such a sight. I heard Debbie and Bobby arguing about it before Bobby angrily left the apartment. After he was gone Debbie crept into my room, lifted me from the bed, and brought me to the couch. First fastening the chain on the door, she turned on the television and found some cartoons. I couldn't see very well through my swollen eyes but the sounds of the outside world were comforting. Debbie brought ice wrapped in a wet towel and gently set it across my face. The sudden bitter cold stung for only an instant before the pain began to subside. I fell into a deep sleep listening to the television and Debbie's sobs.

A knock on the door scared me awake. I sat up painfully and the wet towel fell to my lap, my eyes barely able to make out the door in front of me. The knock sounded again. Standing up slowly I saw the chain hanging from the wall. I was home

alone. I walked to the door and asked, "Who's there."

"It's me, from downstairs," said a kind, sweet voice I recognized from sitting for weeks at her side.

I opened the door and in her shabby dress she held out a kitten, not my kitten, but another that I recognized from all the days sitting by the box full of them. She spoke quietly and evenly when she said, "You lost something."

My appearance did not seem to shock or surprise her. She, like most of the occupants of the building, understood what was going on in our apartment but made no mention. Aside from the constant noise there was a lot of traffic in and out of the place. She must have somehow seen or become aware of the dead kitten behind the building. After some mumbled protestation on my part she insisted I take the new kitten.

After she left I did my best to nuzzle the kitten as carefully as possible so it didn't run off or bite my

swollen face. But my face was too sore and I was too weak to control the young animal that was unaccustomed to being held. The kitten leapt from my hand s to the couch to the floor and scurried throughout the apartment. Stumbling around I chased it without success. The frightened kitten ran into the kitchen and between the refrigerator and the stove. There it stayed, singing its sorrowful kitten cry for the world to hear. Panicking I grabbed the broom from the other side of the refrigerator and tried blindly to find the kitten.

The kitten stopped crying and it made it more difficult to locate. Fumbling around trying to get the new kitten free Bobby walks through the door. I turn to face him but my expression of guilt and fear are masked by the swelling. Finding me digging behind the oven with the broom he half smiles, "Glad someone 'round here's cleaning this shithole."

At the sound of the voice the kitten starts its song again. Bobby was on me before I knew it. He grabbed the broom from my hands and swung it sideways connecting with the back of my head. "That bitch mother a' yours aint here to protect you this time boy. You tryin to hide that fuckin cat from me? Dat what you doin'? Think you can hide that fuckin' cat in my house and I aint gonna know it." His words spewed out in a flurry of contempt as he swung the broom at my already battered body. The kitten continued crying. "This where it is boy? You gonna hide behind the stove like I aint gonna know? Dis my fuckin' stove mufucka," with those words he grabbed the oven with both hands and ripped it from the wall, exposing the balled up kitten. I stood in front of the refrigerator having narrowly escaped being crushed by the toppled oven.

He stepped over the oven to grab the kitten. This time he wrenched the kitten up with his fist tightly around its neck. The kitten stopped crying, then

stopped breathing in Bobby's large, leathered hand. Stepping back over the oven he grabbed my throat with his free hand and again dragged me over to the window. The kitten and I dangling helplessly from our flimsy necks, we made it to the window under a flurry of threats and insults. My head was ringing from the pain I couldn't hear much of what was said but I tried to pay close attention. Again he made me watch as he sent the dead kitten soaring through the afternoon sky.

Heaving me up by the neck with both hands he held my head out of the open window. He put his face against my ear and snarled, "If I see one more gotdamn animal in dis house YOU will be goin' out dis window wit' it."

He pulled me back into the apartment, slammed the window closed, and threw me to floor. As I lay in a pile of tenderized flesh I told myself that I would get a cat as soon as I was able and I would always have a cat and I'd treat it well.

Chapter Seven
My Bodyguard

"Have I got a gift for you," my principal said, as she approached me in the hall.

It was 7 AM, and I was waiting for my students to arrive. "Great, you know I always enjoy a new challenge. What's his name?"

A devious smile crept across her face. "Kendra!"

"A girl?" my displeasure was apparent in my tone.

"Yup, she's been in our system for less than a week and was terrorizing the school from day one. Yesterday she attacked a girl in gym class and hurt her pretty badly." She passed me a photocopied registration form. "Her mom's in prison. She just moved here to live with her auntie. According to her transfer sheet, she's been moving around a lot, going from relative to relative."

I took in this new development for a moment. "When's she coming?"

"She's on the bus right now. She starts today. The Director of Schools wants her with you." She spoke as if offering a compliment.

I took a deep breath. "Yes ma'am. I'll take care of her."

"I know you will." She turned to walk away. With her back to me, she waved and chimed, "Good luck."

Females in a behavior program had historically been an issue for me because the classes are usually full of pubescent boys, as my class was at the time. I stood by the door with a new trepidation. The first bus pulled up, and I walked out the double glass doors, positioning a doorstop to hold one door open, so I wouldn't be locked out. The bus stopped, and the door opened as I approached.

"Good morning, Mr. Love, got a new one for ya," said the affable bus driver.

"I heard," I replied, doing my best to sound cheerful.

"She's a pistol. She's already started in with the boys. Be careful," she warned.

"Yes ma'am. Thank you ma'am." I said, biting my tongue.

The boys filed off, and I greeted each one with a friendly "Good morning Sir" and I got the same in return. Finally a hesitant young woman appeared at the front of the bus. She took one slow step down, then another. She stopped, and we were eye to eye as she stood on the last step of the bus. We were sizing each other up. I immediately noticed the cross hanging from her neck. This particular cross is a craft commonly made by prison inmates.

Pointing to the cross braided from thin white string I asked softly, "Did your mother make that for you?"

Her scowl turned to confusion, "Yeah," she said and dropped her guard.

"I have one just like it at home. My brother made it for me." I extended my hand, "My name's Mr.

Love and I prefer 'Yes Sir' to 'yeah'. Why don't you hop in at the back of the line?"

"Yes Sir," she replied as she gripped my hand, holding it tightly as she stepped from the bus.

I waved to the bus driver and moved on to the front of my line of students as the bus drove off. I raised my arm and directed my line to class. I found a desk and a set of books for Kendra and waited patiently until all of my students had arrived. When everyone was present and seated, I introduced our new student, and we proceeded to go over the rules. The boys had already noticed her. She was a tall, pretty young woman, and the boys were unsettled by her presence among them. The day progressed along at a slow clip until Michael became frustrated with me and exploded in anger. Before I responded to the boy's outburst, Kendra was out of her seat and had let her own anger explode across Michael's face. She stepped back and stood facing the room of stunned boys.

"Any a' ya'll got anything else to say about Mr. Love?" Her voice was threatening and ruthless. The boys shrank in their chairs without a word. "Kendra, I know you're new, but in my class you are not allowed to get out of your seat without permission. Please go back to your seat." I said coolly.

"Yes Sir. Sorry Sir." She said smoothly as she strode back to her seat.

The pace of the day hastened after Kendra's unexpected infusion of energy. Before I knew it, it was time for lunch. Everyone lined up, and the boy closest to Michael started teasing him about being hit by a girl.

Michael's response came nervously, "Yo, she strong, G. I didn't see *you* get up in her face when she was in front of *you*."

"Shoot, she aint stronger than me. I'll kick that girl's ass." As the words came out of his mouth Kendra's fist smashed into the back of the boy's

head. The boy collapsed to the ground, holding his head in loud sobs.

"Sir, you can not use profanity in my class," I said to the huddled mass on my floor. "Please Sir step back into line. Or if you'd prefer I'll call someone to come and get you if you're too injured to move." I tried to keep the sarcasm from my voice. The boy stood up and took his spot in line. I stood in the hallway by my door as my assistant led the line out of the class. When Kendra was in front of me I held my arm up to stop her as the line proceeded down the hall.

I spoke quietly, "I appreciate you being so cooperative this morning. You're a very intelligent young woman. Your work is nearly perfect. However, I can't have you beating up my class. At this rate, there will be no one left in class after you've sent them all to the hospital. Does that make sense?"

"Yes Sir, I was just defending you. These boys are stupid and need some sense beat into them." She

was very confident, and I was surprised by her maturity.

Though I tried not to laugh at her comment, my face broke and I let out a laugh, "Well ma'am, you may be right about that, but believe me, I've dealt with much tougher things in my life than these boys. I can defend myself without violence, and I hope in our time together you'll learn the same. Cool?"

Her brilliant smile warmed my soul, "Yes Sir."

"Cool, let's get to lunch. This place has a pretty good cafeteria" I held up my arm in the direction of the cafeteria, and we walked down the hall, quietly comparing notes about foster care and having a mother in prison. As I opened up to her, she stood up straighter and held herself with even more confidence.

Kendra turned out to be a perfect addition to the class, a foil to the boys who saw themselves as indestructible and untamable. She was smart, witty, strong, and unimaginably fast. She

challenged the boys to do their best, so they might one day be better than her. The boys rose to her challenge, and in the process unknowingly exceeded my own expectations. When they couldn't outsmart her academically, each boy tried and failed to get the best of her in a physical confrontation. Her fighting style was fierce and unfamiliar to the boys. She fought with a control the boys did not know or understand.

After only a few days, she had established herself at the head of the class. The pecking order had been disrupted, and the change impacted the entire class. Because of Kendra's enthusiasm to learn, it was suddenly cool for the boys to read, to study, and to learn. Just as her demeanor changed the attitudes of the boys, her own attitude changed as well. As she established her place among the fold in our nurturing environment, she blossomed into a whole new person. Her attitude change manifested into a personality change. Her usual attire of short black

t-shirts, too tight jeans, and platform sneakers adorned with hand drawn graffiti complimented by extension-filled hair gave way to more modest casual dress and natural hair. Only the string cross remained. Privately she confessed her newly found happiness and the comfort she felt in her new school.

In the short time she was with us, Kendra's transformation was noticed by and commented on by the students, faculty, administration, and most importantly her. She was pleased with herself and asked me on more than one occasion if I thought her mother would be proud of her. Experience with the same emotionally charged question prompted the impulsive inquiry, "Have you written to her and told her about yourself and all that you've done since you've lived here?" The question seemed to puzzle more than upset her, "I write to her all the time in my journal." "Yes, but do you mail the letters you write? You didn't answer my question. Have you told her

about yourself, this you, the new you, the calm, studious you?"

"I don't know what that last word means, Sir." She said flatly.

"Studious, it means hard working as in school work, as in 'you are a studious worker in class'." I tried to explain in a manner she would understand.

"No Sir. But I think if I told her that she would be mad that I was trying to talk over her. I couldn't use that word in a letter to my mother." She looked embarrassed, so I tried to be reassuring in my response.

"I couldn't use that word in a letter to my biological mother either. She wouldn't have been mad but she would have never known what it meant, and she wouldn't have thought to look it up I'm sure. But you know what, you can write to her and not use that word. Just tell her how you're doing, and tell her that you're happy even though you miss her. Definitely mention the

cross." I pointed to the cross still dangling from her neck. "You can write in class as a grammar assignment. I won't read the letters, but I will stamp and mail them for you," I offered, trying to inspire a connection between the young woman and her absent mother.

"I have to admit that I'm a little jealous of you." I confessed.

"*You're* jealous of *me*? Why?" Her confusion was evident.

"When I was your age, I wasn't allowed to write to my mother, and I missed her just as much as you miss your mom. I wasn't in foster care with family like you are, and I know that your situation is not perfect and it doesn't make you 100 percent happy all of the time, but you're with family. The state decided that I couldn't have contact with my biological family when I was in foster care, and to be honest I think that just made it worse." My eyes got wet but a tear did not fall. Kendra's face

let me know that she understood what I was trying to say.

Then she began to cry. Quiet burning tears ran down her face. I fought the impulse to give her a hug as the climate of schools had changed so drastically since I was a kid. Not many teachers, myself included, felt comfortable hugging students. I pulled my cell phone from my pocket and called Michelle on her phone. She was in the classroom next door, and I asked her to come over and provide an escape route for Kendra. After gaining her trust at the outset, I worked hard and convinced Kendra that Michelle and Renee were also trustworthy confidants. In our tiny microcosm we had established a support network of honest adults that the kids knew were unconditionally trustworthy. For these children, honest and trustworthy adults were hard to come by.

Kendra's stay with us was brief, yet monumental. She changed a lot of perceptions, including my

own. She was my first truly positive, confrontation-free experience with a female student in an alternative behavior setting. The boys had grown to respect and even rely on her for her academic and athletic skill. If ever I were occupied with another student, the boys would turn to Kendra for help without question and without having to ask my permission. One morning Kendra didn't step off the bus, and I went to the office to see if her aunt had called. I was duly informed that she had been withdrawn the previous afternoon after school. I grieved silently as I walked back to class to inform the boys. They took the news uncharacteristically well, as most of them did not deal well with change. Later it occurred to me that her being withdrawn after school saved us all a hard goodbye, and in my mind I thanked her aunt for her kind gesture.

Several months after she had transferred out of school, I received a letter from Kendra addressed

to me at school. I was hesitant to open it since she was withdrawn so abruptly. Curiosity got the better of me, and I zipped a pen through the top of the envelope ripping through the seal. Unfolding the single page, I ached with anxiety before I read it through. Her handwriting was more elegant and flowing, her writing not as fluid as I knew it could be. Smiling and relieved, I got everyone's attention and read the letter to the class.

Dear Mr. Love,

I wanted to write to you and the class to say hello. I like my new school and my teachers are nice. I am not in an alternative school. I don't even know if they have one here. I miss all of you and I hope I can visit some time soon. I am still living with my auntie. She got a new job that's why we had to move. I have been writing to my mom and she writes back. My mom gets out of prison soon and my auntie said she might come and live with

us. I hope she does. Do you still write letters to your brother? Is he still in prison?

Thank you for being so nice to me and respecting me and helping me all the time. You were the first teacher who was ever nice to me. And the first teacher I ever liked cuz you always called me ma'am. I like my teachers in my new school but they're not nice like you. We don't talk about the same stuff we did but it's regular school so I guess it's different.

Please tell everyone I said hello. They can write back if they want. You can write back too.

Bye for now,

Kendra

Chapter Eight
The Betrayal

It was the middle of February 1979 when Bobby gave Matthew and me each a dollar and sent us to the store. Matthew was to buy whatever he wanted, while I was to buy a TV Guide for Bobby. He was too high to go himself and high enough to let me out of the apartment. *Roots: The Next Generations* was set to air, and Bobby wanted to know when. We walked to the closest store a few blocks away. I handed my dollar to the man behind the counter, as I placed the small magazine on the counter. Matthew waited by the door, already drinking his bottle of Malta, a malt soft drink common among the people of the Village. Debbie often snuck it to me in place of real food when Bobby refused to let me eat. The thick dark drink was filling like a meal, an acquired taste, but delicious once you had enough of it. While Matthew loaded his pockets with candy, I waited for my change. Once it was in my

hand, I stuffed it into my pocket and headed toward home, trailing Matthew by a few paces. He did not like to walk with me, especially when he had candy. It was nearly pointless to ask him to share, but I always begged anyway. This time was no different. All the way to the apartment, I hobbled behind him, begging for some of his candy. His laugh was his refusal, as he washed down his candy with the cold Malta.

When we entered the apartment, I placed the TV Guide on the kitchen table, and with a cold hand pulled Bobby's change from my pocket. Matthew sat on the couch announcing our arrival that had gone unnoticed. Bobby hugged Matthew to him with a wicked grin. I stood silently still in the kitchen, waiting for permission to move.

"Bring me my TV Guide and my change." Bobby shouted at the television.

I brought him what he asked for and handed it to him from as far away as I could stand. He smiled as he flipped through the TV Guide, the change

nestled in his grip. Closing the magazine, he opened his palms and counted the coins. His fingers tightened around the money.

"Where's the rest? What else did you buy?" He growled, staring at his fist.

"I got the TV Guide and took the change the guy gave me and put it in my pocket. I didn't buy anything. You can ask Matthew." I pleaded.

"I aint askin' him. I'm askin' YOU. What else did you buy? A TV Guide cost 25 cents. I only got 60 some-odd cents here. So, what else did you buy?" His slurred voice wavered as he emphasized his words.

His rise from the couch was slow and telegraphed but escape was impossible. The impending beating threw me across the living room, but I had no other answer to the question he repeated as he tossed me around the room. When his patience ran out, he grabbed his coat and dragged me from the apartment and down to the store where I'd bought the magazine.

Bobby tossed me at the counter and I knocked my head into a large jar of loose pickles. The clerk looked across the counter in shock. Bobby pulled my hair and showed my face to the man and began his tirade.

"Wha' did little bastard buy when he was in here a minute ago?" Bobby screamed.

"Relax man. Leave the kid alone. Yeah, he was in here. He bought a TV Guide and left with some other kid. A bigger, blonde headed kid. The blonde kid bought a bunch a candy." The clerk said nervously.

"Then where's the rest of my change," Bobby said, opening up his hand to reveal the coins I had given him.

"Hey man, relax. TV Guide's 35 cents. The kid gave me a dollar. That's the right change." The man at the register looked around to the other customers in the line and pulled a TV Guide from the small rack on the countertop, pointing

out the price on the cover. Bobby's anger turned to irritation.

"Next time I wanna receipt. Got me walkin' all day-- way down here in the gotdamn cold. Get the hell outta here," he demanded and swung me by the hair toward the doorway. I heard someone yell at Bobby, something about calling the police. Holding onto the door, ready to leave, I watched Bobby turn and swing wildly at an older man. His stupor did not allow him to connect and the older man scolded Bobby and told him to leave. Bobby walked to the door and pushed me outside back into the cold. As we walked hurriedly through the cold, he warned me of the beating I had waiting for me when we got home.

Later that night, a loud banging on the door and the word "Police" shook the apartment alive. Frantically, Debbie burst into our room and told Matthew and me to sit on the couch. She coached us to repeat the usual story of our regular fights and sibling rivalry to explain my cuts and

bruises. Meanwhile, Bobby moved in silence, transferring all of the drugs into their bedroom. After the last trip, he sat on the couch with the rest of us. We all then pretended to watch television.

From the couch I heard the pounding more clearly, followed by a loud commanding voice: "Open up, Bridgeport Police."

With the apartment acceptably presentable, Debbie opened the door as far as the chain would allow. She spoke with the officers in a low voice, then closed the door and undid the chain to reopen the door. Four officers entered the apartment in single file. Bobby stood up in a defensive stance. The police were not a familiar presence in the Village but had been to our apartment on several occasions.

The officers questioned Bobby about the incident at the store. From the couch, I heard that the clerk had called the police about a disturbance and possible child abuse. An officer stooped in

front of Matthew and I while the others stood surrounding Bobby and Debbie in the kitchen.

"Did he hurt you in the store," the officer asked me pointing to Bobby.

"No," I answered softly.

"Did he hurt you after you left the store," he asked.

"No." Bobby had taught me after our first interaction with the police to only answer the question I was asked, and to never give more information than necessary.

"Does he ever hurt you?" The officer continued.

"No." I answered.

"Does he ever hurt you?" The officer asked Matthew who was sitting beside me.

"No," he said with a laugh.

Surprised by his lack of concern, the officer asked, "What's so funny about that?"

"No one hurts *me*. We fight all the time, and I win. That's all we do is fight." Matthew's excitement was nearly uncontainable.

"Is that true? Do you two fight much?" The officer asked.

I turned to Matthew with disdain, "Yes, but I beat *him* one time."

"Just one time," Matthew blurted in annoyance.

"Did he," pointing to Matthew, "do *this*" pointing back to my face, "to you?" The officer asked.

"Yes," I replied as Matthew gave a short laugh. The officer stood up and walked to the kitchen to confer with the other officers. There was a hushed discussion, and the officers walked to the door. The officer that had spoken with Matthew and I turned and called to Matthew, "Hey, son, be nicer to your little brother. He's your brother. You need to be protecting him, not hurting him." Debbie opened the door and let the officers out. Debbie went into the kitchen and waited by the edge of the window. "They're gone," she said finally.

"Good job boys. Damn good job. Dumb mufuckas think they gon' come up in 'ere and say

some shit to me? Shit!" Bobby said triumphantly as he paced in front of the door. The officers' visit had sobered him up, and his speech was clear and condescending. "Baby, get my shit and cook us up," he ordered. Debbie moved quickly toward the bedroom.

"You two go to yo room and play," he instructed, waving a burning cigarette at us. We got up quickly. Bobby called Matthew over to him. I walked into the hall and waited closest to the edge, where I was out of sight of Bobby and Matthew.

"You did a great job, son. I'm proud of you. Stay out here with us. You can watch TV with us." He said cheerfully. I moved on down the hall to the bedroom.

Several weeks later, the police returned, accompanied by a social worker I had seen before. They interviewed Debbie in the kitchen. Debbie held Ruby in her arms to give the appearance of being a loving mother. The police

walked through the apartment, inspecting each room in turn from Ruby's small, toy-filled room to the bathroom. Matthew and I were interviewed separately in our bedroom by the social worker with a police officer standing guard. She asked about the incident at the store, and I repeated the story of the officers' visit later that same night. She asked about fighting with Matthew and if anyone else ever hurt me. I told her that the boys in the neighborhood often beat me up and that Matthew and me fought all the time: all things I had been coached to say. The visitors left before Bobby came home, but when he did arrive, Debbie told him what had transpired. He was angry until he spoke with Matthew and me and heard our versions of what had happened and what we had said. He dismissed me without comment but congratulated Matthew and spoke of the pride he had for his son.

It was March 20, 1979 when the police returned, this time accompanied by more social workers. Bobby and Debbie were both home. The social worker who had interviewed us earlier explained that they were temporarily taking Matthew out of the house, as it had been determined that I was unsafe with Matthew in the home. Upon hearing their words, I collapsed in tears and frustration. My grief was irrepressible. I begged them not to take Matthew, but they all assured me it was for only a little while. They promised I would be back together with my brother in no time at all. My crying and pleas got louder and more incomprehensible. I couldn't explain that what I really wanted was to be taken away myself without having to explain why. The social workers and the police officers all tried to calm me, but there was no consolation for the betrayal I felt. The police, the social workers, and the teachers at school: I was sure they all knew what was happening, but they left me and took the

favored son away. I was more frightened than I had ever been when the door finally closed and Matthew was gone.

I ran to my room and closed the door. Collapsing on my bed, I tried to stifle my tears, but they only came harder. Debbie entered my room and sat on the bed, rubbing my back. Her voice was shaky, and her words were incongruous with her quivering body. She tried to assure me, like the police and the social workers, that everything was going to be all right. The words only intensified my fear, as I thought about being home alone with Bobby.

The torment I feared never came. With Matthew gone, it became apparent that there was no one to blame for my disturbingly battered appearance. The daily beatings ended immediately. Bobby's kindness that was so frequently showered upon Matthew now transferred to me. He brought me with him everywhere he went, in and out of the Village.

One night we sang "Y.M.C.A." by the Village People over and over at the top of our voices as we drove a stolen van to a drug buy. He sat me on his lap and let me "steer" the giant vehicle on the way to buy. Sitting in the van waiting for him to return, I listened to the radio, drank Yoo-hoo, and ate pizza.

Bobby bought me candy and Yoo-hoo nearly each day. I was allowed to play outside as spring approached and the weather became warmer. Being seen with Bobby had brought a certain level of protection among the neighborhood children. I could walk and play outside without fear. I made friends with several of the other kids and was allowed to visit them in their apartments. My body healed and my appearance became less unsettling.

Debbie also went unharmed while Matthew was gone. Bobby's rage was all but gone, and because she too escaped the beatings, she was able to turn more tricks outside the apartment. Bobby and I

sat on the couch and watched television, smoking pot and drinking beer, while Debbie worked her nights away. Debbie was more attentive to the cleanliness of the apartment, and the refrigerator always had food. The calm of the apartment was palpable.

We laughed and had a good time around the apartment. Each day I ate hot meals at the table with Debbie, Bobby, and Ruby in her high chair. Debbie bought an ear-piercing gun for Ruby's first birthday, and I was allowed to sit with Debbie and her "friends" as they tried to figure out how to use it. I was allowed to play with and even feed Ruby for the first time while Matthew was away. Since she had been born almost a year earlier, I had been kept away from her, as I was so despised by Bobby. He didn't want "Debbie's bastard kid" near his own child, though Debbie was the mother of both of us.

Four weeks went by, and each week was better than the last. We were like a real family whenever

the social workers came by. I was noticeably happier and more relaxed than ever. Each time the social worker got up to go, she would comment on how pleasant we all seemed and what a change she had noticed since first coming to the apartment. She was very pleased with our progress as a family, and she was convinced it was Matthew who had caused me so much harm. She gave us weekly updates on Matthew who was living with an older woman who had had years of experience with foster children. According to the reports Matthew was doing well.

She said he seemed happy and settled, but that it was time that he come home, so we could all be together again. I pleaded with the social worker as I had when she had originally taken Matthew, but this time because I didn't want the happiness to end. I did not fear the future. I had gotten a taste of Matthew's relationship with Bobby, and I didn't want it to end. It was plain to me why Matthew was so happy with Bobby. Unwilling to

give up the relationship that had formed between us all, I continued to beg the social worker to keep Matthew away. She refuted my pleas by suggesting that Matthew was a calm and happy boy. She promised that he would not cause me any more problems. Knowing I could never tell the truth, I stopped pleading and sat quietly by my mother's side. The social worker told us that Matthew would be returning home in a few days and that we should all prepare ourselves for his return.

On April 18, Matthew returned home with an unfamiliar suitcase. He was accompanied by the same social worker that had been visiting us, but there were no police officers as there had been when Matthew had left. His suitcase was full of new clothes and toys that he pulled out and displayed to us excitedly. He was exuberant to be back in the apartment, and Bobby and Debbie were giving him a hero's welcome. There was a cake, laughter, and group hugs. I sat on the couch

and sulked, knowing the good times were over. The social worker scolded me for not joining in the revelry and suggested that Matthew and I attend counseling sessions to work out our differences. She offered to set it all up, but Debbie declined in favor of first "seeing how it goes." The social worker left happier than I had ever seen her.

Evening came and Debbie tried to stay in to be with Matthew. Bobby became angry at her short-lived refusal to work. As she went out the door dressed in her street clothes, I knew that everything would be back to normal soon. I sat on the couch watching TV with Matthew, as I had with Bobby while Matthew was gone. Bobby came over to the couch with a smoldering joint. In a motion I mistook for generosity, Bobby's hand came down and pushed me off the couch. He handed the joint to Matthew and spoke while holding his breath, "I bet that old bitch didn't give you any of this in'at foster home." He

coughed out a short burst of laughter as the air filled with smoke. I sat on the floor, looking at the two of them on the couch with disdain. They passed the joint back and forth between them a few times before Bobby put it into an ashtray on the coffee table next to me. It was then he seemed to notice me.

"Get us a couple of beers." He instructed. I hopped up quickly and returned with three bottles of beer. Bobby took all three, opened two and put the third between his legs. He handed one of the open bottles to Matthew.

"Welcome home son," he said to Matthew holding his bottle up in Matthew's direction. Matthew held up his own bottle and clinked it against Bobby's. Speechless, I stood staring at the two of them.

"What da fuck you lookin at? Damn boy, aint you got somethin' ta do? Get the fuck outta here. Go play with yer toys or somethin'." With a wave of

his bottle I was dismissed, and order returned to the apartment.

Chapter Nine
Reading on the Block

Time passed quickly for me at the JDC under Tre's guidance. I felt at ease in my new position after only a few weekends on the job. Soon enough, I felt like I'd been there for years, although I began to notice minute details that no one seemed to know, notice, or really care about, particularly the Center's library. The library consisted of a two-foot by five-foot "locker" half-filled with over-worn paperback books nearly as old as me. There were no guidelines as to what the kids could read. We passed out books as kids requested them, though few seemed interested in the books they were given. However, some of the kids seemed truly interested in reading, even if just to kill time.

I had begun collecting books long ago. My personal classroom library was full of books of all reading levels that I had picked out to secretly coax reluctant readers into becoming avid

readers. Picture books were an especially useful tool in this area. While my students of all ages would poke fun at my having picture books, they would inevitably grab one at some point to try to understand why I found them so fascinating. I also made a regular practice of presenting picture books in class – even to a room full of high school students.

After one especially insightful conversation on the block, I brought in a copy of Tookie Williams's "The Tookie Protocol For Peace," a renunciation of violence printed from Tookie's website. I brought it to give to a young Crip who had told me he wanted to quit "the life" when he got out. The life he referred to was the life of gang banging and hustling that had brought him back and forth to Detention for years. Unsure as to the guidelines, I first gave it to my Sergeant and asked her if it was within regulations to give a detainee reading material printed from the Internet. She asked me why, so I showed her

what I had brought and explained why I had brought it. After a quizzical perusal of the unbound pages, she told me she didn't care what I gave them to read, as long as it wasn't a magazine or anything else with staples.

I thanked her quickly and let the papers rest on the desk for several minutes, trying not to seem too eager to take it up on the block. At dinnertime I walked upstairs to pass out trays, and I nonchalantly passed the pages through the bars to the young man and said, "I'm not really sure about this, or if someone might give you hassle over it, but if so just tell whoever it is that I gave it to you."

After pulling his tray beneath the cell door he flipped through the pages quickly. He looked up at me, and gave me an eager, "Thank you Sir." When I walked by his cell a moment later after passing out more trays, I saw him sitting on his bunk with his tray on his lap reading while he ate. My excitement ran rampant, as I wondered what

type of reaction he would have. When I returned to pick up his tray, I saw that he was only on the second page. I realized that I had no idea as to what his reading level might be, so I asked, "Slow going?" I kept moving as I spoke.

"No Sir." He responded, as he stood up and approached the bars. His voice followed me down the block as I collected more trays. "I've read it a couple of times already. I'm trying to memorize it."

"Memorize what?" A voice from an adjoining cell asked.

"Man, Mr. Love gave me this thing by Tookie Williams, and I'm gonna memorize it. It's cool, man."

"Yo, Mr. Love, Sir, you know who Tookie Williams is?" Another voice asked in disbelief.

"Was, Sir. Tookie is dead now. California executed him a few years ago this month actually." I said matter-of-factly.

"Mr. Love, how you know Tookie Williams?" The same young man asked.

I looked at him and replied with a smirk, "Sir, I may be white, but I'm not stupid. Tookie Williams is probably THE most famous man in gang culture. I wouldn't be me if I didn't know who he was."

"You a Crip, Mr. Love?" He asked.

"No Sir, I'm a teacher." I responded flatly.

"You know what I mean Sir," he said with a smile.

"Yes Sir, I do know what you mean, but we both know that discussing gangs and gang affiliation is against rules, and I take my job and the rules very seriously." I said as I carried my armful of trays up the block.

"Mr. Love, Sir, do you have any other books by Tookie?" The young man asked politely.

"I only have one book by Tookie Williams Sir," I shot back as I stepped off the block. I could hear

the voices buzzing behind me. I had peaked their interest. Again.

The next weekend I brought them books from my home and classroom libraries. I brought some standard young adult classics like <u>Bud, Not Buddy</u>, <u>The Outsiders</u>, <u>Hatchet</u>, and <u>Maniac Magee</u>, in addition to some of my personal favorites, <u>Dangerous Angels</u>, <u>The Count of Monte Cristo</u>, <u>The Little Prince</u>, <u>The Alchemist</u>, but no book proved more popular than Tookie's prison-scribed memoir <u>Blue Rage, Black Redemption</u>. The boys were not used to reading, and they required a lot of encouragement. I told them that the books I loved most were the ones that I had to start a few different times before I really got into, but once I got far enough in, I was hooked.

"Give a book a chance, and if you need to put it down until later, let it rest, and give it another chance," I told them all repeatedly. "My rule is if I'm not into it by the first 50 pages, I'm probably

not going to get into it. If I put it down before that, I'll make a mental note to pick it back up later until I've gotten through the first 50. Then I make my final decision; if it's any good, the choice is made for me, and I just keep reading. The more you read, you'll make up your own rule."

"Time stands still in here. I know that. Books will not just take up your time, but they'll take you outta *here*." I said waving my outstretched arms around indicating the bars and the cinderblock walls.

"So if I read this book you'll let me outta here Sir?" the young man said hopefully.

"No Sir, that's not what I mean. A good book will take you beyond these walls, beyond your world and into the world of your book. It will take your mind to places you've never imagined." I replied.

"Are there any books we can read that *will* get us outta here? I mean for real." Another young man hollered out down the block.

"I'm sorry Sir, but no." I said a little despondently.

The kids read more after being given books that interested them. Many of them started reading any book they could get their hands on. They began to ask for specific titles and subjects. We talked about what type of books I had and then started bringing books they requested that I had in my library. Only from my teaching experience was I able to recognize that the reading levels of numerous detainees increased. Cellmates and neighbors would convince each other to get involved in reading to make use of their time. Reading had transformed the way many of the young men spent their time. They were no longer just doing time, but spending their time on something they had learned to enjoy.

Each night all of the detainees were allotted one hour of TV time in which they came out of their cells and sat together in a common area to watch television. Some took this opportunity to play

cards as well, but all of them used the time to socialize with other kids they normally did not see. During one such hour, I overheard some guys planning to perform car crashes as soon as the lights were turned off at 10:00 PM. Car crashes were common activities in Detention, especially after lights out. The boys would climb onto the metal shelf built into the back wall of the cell, and jump onto their bunks below. The sound of a body slamming onto the wall-mounted metal bunk resonating through the block resembled the sound of two cars colliding. The guys were the main culprits of this activity. They performed car crashes after lights out because it was easier to do it anonymously, though it did happen during the day. The consequence of such activities varied in severity, but mainly the consequence required a lot of paperwork. As with every activity in the Detention Center or anywhere else, an ounce of prevention is worth hours of paperwork.

After escorting the guys back up to their cells and unshackling everyone, I walked back off the block and headed around the corner. Pulling a chair from the watch desk, I returned to the block carrying the chair. I positioned the chair in the middle of the block and made myself comfortable.

I pulled a book from one of my large cargo pockets, cleared my throat, and began reading aloud from Adrian McKinty's excellent crime novel, <u>Dead I Well May Be</u>. There was talking on the block as I began, but I was used to reading to large groups who didn't want to listen. When reading to my classes, I often used accents and a variety of voices to bring stories to life, so with an Irish accent I started in. Unfamiliar with an officer reading to them, the boys closest to me began shushing the others around them. Soon the only sound on the block was my accented voice booming through the block. I waited for any objections, but none came.

Behind my head, I heard the black box on the wall squeal. It was the audio monitor being activated from downstairs. Instantly I knew the Sergeant was listening in on me. She listened for several minutes, and then the hum went away, indicating that she was done. No one came to stop me. When another officer appeared on the block, I continued reading, expecting to be told to stop, but he had only come to "run the clock." The "watchman's clock," a monitoring device that we all wore at some point, was used for safety checks that we had to do every thirty minutes, all day long. "Watch tours" required an officer to use a key located at the end of each block to timestamp a wheel of paper inside the clock. To my surprise, the officer merely squeezed by me, making his rounds without a word or even a glance.

The guys sat on their bunks listening intently, as I read the adventures of Michael Forsythe. They were deeply enthralled by his criminal world. The

reading was soon punctuated by cheerful exclamations, hoots and hollers from the guys in their cells. Their responses of uninhibited enthusiasm made the reading interactive and thoroughly engaging. When the call came for "lights out," they all begged for more. It was Friday night, and everyone knew I'd be back tomorrow. I told them that if they stayed calm all night, I'd come back up tomorrow and read some more. Though they begged me not to stop, they all agreed, and the block was quiet all night. The next night when I appeared on the block, everyone greeted me with a reminder of my promise. I was as true to my word as they were, and I spent all of my down time on their block reading to my captive audience. Again they protested for "just one more chapter" when "lights out" was called. Again I told them that if they remained calm, I would read to them the next day. The attention-starved young men responded enthusiastically by listening actively

when engaged with positive adult attention. The importance of our reading sessions became clear later that night when a car crash was heard. The typically tight-lipped crew to whom I had been reading was eager to point out that the disturbance had come from the opposite block. The reading of the book continued, even though I only worked weekends at the time. I read whenever I had the chance after that first reading. I had to travel around to each of the four male blocks to read because, as of my first reading, the original crew had been split up onto the other blocks for one reason or another. I traveled around, finishing the book for some and hitting points in the middle or end for others. It took nearly six shifts to read the whole book to the original set of boys. When it was over, I mentioned that there were two other books in the series, and the guys begged to have them. In the end, I bought a set for the library, so they could read and share them at their leisure.

Reading <u>Dead I Well May Be</u> brought my relationship with the guys to a different level. There now existed the intimacy of a classroom, but on a larger scale. The guys and I had honest discussions about books and their characters, plots, and morals. Every week I brought in more books, and every book led to more in-depth discussions: taking responsibility, having babies with young girls to have someone to love, "baby momma drama," how bad visits led to bad behavior on the block, being honest with yourself, and loving yourself before you can love someone else. The young men approached me with all of these topics and insights after reading one book or another. It all started by trying to deter an evening filled with car crashes and paperwork. One night on the block, as I ran my clock, a young man I'd spoken to frequently about books asked, "Mista Love, why you like readin' so much?"

"Cuz he a teacher, stupid!" A voice yelled from down the block.

Grabbing onto the bars and leaning his head in the direction of the voice, the first boy called back, "Man, shut up. I aint talkin' to you." He stepped back but kept his hands firmly on the bars, his knuckles turning a paler shade of brown as his grip tightened. He faced me and awaited my answer.

"Well Sir, when I was young I didn't have such a great home life. My teachers at school knew that I was afraid to go home, so they would let me stay at school. They didn't really have anything for me to do, so they would just feed me books. As I grew up, my life became increasingly unstable and out of control, so books became my haven. I was always safe reading a book. I was always busy reading a book, and reading books kept me out of a lot of trouble." I felt my eyes welling up as I spoke. Thinking back on the times I hid in school,

too afraid to go home, was something I tried not to think about.

"Sir, is that why you became a teacher, cuz a' teachers you had?" he asked respectfully.

"In a way, yes Sir I did. In the end though, I became a teacher because I felt I needed to help kids. I wanted to help kids. And I knew I could help kids as a teacher."

"That why you workin' here now? You tryin' to help us too?" He asked with a bit of sarcasm.

"Do you think I'm helping you?" Answering his question with a question.

"You be helpin' me a lot more if you open dis cell and let me out." He replied with a smile. The block erupted with cheers and a chorus of "Let me out too!" from nearly every cell.

"Sir, if I could I would, and I hope when the time comes I *will* be the one to open your cell to let you go home." I said earnestly.

"Nah, fa real doe, Mista Love. You be helpin' us out all the time. I see how you be runnin' da clock

and you always be getting' us books an' stuff when we ask an' everyone else jus' be sayin' dey be gettin' stuff when dey get aroun' to it." His voice had lost its earlier sarcasm, and his sincerity cut through the bars and my façade. I excused myself and moved to the top of the block. I made my exit, but not before asking if anyone needed anything. A loud "NO SIR" reverberated up the block. Hastily retreating off the block and into the shower stall, I wiped my eyes out of sight of the omnipresent cameras.

Tearless and calm, I walked downstairs to grab a book for a young man I had spoken to many times before. I had noticed him sitting silently, as I spoke with the other young man a few cells down. He was sitting pensively in his cell, his cellmate having been released earlier in the day. I grabbed a copy of <u>Man's Search for Meaning</u> that I kept in my locker. I knew the young man well, and I knew he was an exceptional reader, even though he didn't attend school regularly

unless he was in Detention. I also knew the charges he was facing and the future he could have. With the book in hand, I approached his cell and passed the book through the bars.

"I see you sitting there. Hiding in the shadows, masking the pain and loneliness of being locked up," I said. The young man's face contorted into an uneasy stare. He stood and approached the bars as he reached for the book. "I can tell by the look on your face that these are not words you expected to hear today." I said as the face pressed against the bars.

"What? You mean you coming up here talking like a guru? No one talks to us like you do. You use big words," he paused, examining me carefully from behind the bars, "but you show us respect." The face confessed.

I let the compliment slide to avoid an awkward conversation about other staff members. "I think you might like this book, but for now just read part one. You can read part two in college," I

said, sure that I was the first person to have ever told him he was going to college.

"Why?" He asked defiantly as if he thought I was insulting his intelligence.

"It has nothing to do with you. It's just that I read the book from cover to cover one time and the second part is all about a very specific area of psychology. The first part, that's the story that I think you need to read."

"A'ight den. But why you think I need to read this one?"

"I'll tell it to you like this. I keep a copy of that book near me all the time. Whenever my life seems rough and I can't take it anymore, I open that book to any page in part one. I read whatever I flip to and I realize that if *that man* can survive *what he went through*, then I can survive whatever *I'm going through*, and it makes my life seem *a whole lot easier*." I spoke quietly as I stood a few inches from the bars. "Take care of yourself.

I'll see you tomorrow Sir." I said as I stepped away.

"Sir," he whispered as he held up the book to me, "Thank you."

"You're welcome Sir. Good night."

"Good night Sir."

Chapter Ten

The Gun

"Get ou' that bed mufucka and get in your gotdamn birthday suit. You got two fuckin minutes to get yo ass out them clothes an in yo birthday suit or I'm aunna kick your fuckin ass. When I come back into this fuckin room you *better fuckin be ready*" Bobby's voice exploding through the night brought the overhead light flooding the room.

I had been sound asleep, didn't know where or what time it was but recognized the command through the blinding light. And I knew to obey. Out of bed pulling off my clothes before the door slams to wake the dead. But it doesn't wake my brother still lying in the bed I scrambled out of. He knew better than to open his eyes and I knew better than to disturb him in any way while getting out of our bed. "Don't wake your brother, he got nothin ta fuckin do wi'this" had been beaten in to me years before.

Bobby had recently taken all of us to get fancy suits to wear to his mother's birthday. This had been very exciting since I only had two pairs of pants and a couple of t-shirts we had gotten from either the Salvation Army or the clothes closet at the welfare office downtown. Since Bobby had paid for our suits we had to keep them on display in a separate part of the closet that was clear of any junk. My suit was to be a constant reminder of how good he was to us and to me especially. How I didn't deserve to live in his house. What it was until that point was a constant reminder of pain.

I hurried out of bed and went to get the suit. I pulled off my bottoms and wrestled my tired limbs into the suit and clipped on my tie. I slid my feet easily into my shiny black shoes that had been bought several sizes too large so I could grow into them. I didn't mind having shoes too large since the sneakers I wore most days were at least one size too small.

I stood by the closet as proud as I ever was. There was no mirror but I knew I looked good. When I'd worn the suit to the birthday party everyone remarked at how cute I looked and it made me feel good. I felt good standing there then. I waited for Bobby to come back in. I knew enough not to leave the room looking for him. He'd told me he'd be back. Swaying as my eyes shut, my body started to shut down from exhaustion. I don't know how long I stood there but I know it had to have been the middle of the night because my body did not want to be awake. As a kid I always wanted to be awake when morning came. Just as I was about to fall over asleep I was knocked to the floor by a heavy hand to the side of my head. I knew better than to fall asleep but my body couldn't help it. I had not heard the door open. I had not heard Bobby enter the room. I knew better than to fall asleep when he had told me to get up.

I planted my hands on the ground and tried to raise myself up to present myself again. I tried to wake myself in my head. It had been only seconds but it felt like hours in those few moments my worn out body was allowed to rest on the floor. My head was ringing and my knees were weak. I propped up on my hands and knees when no sooner came a forceful kick to my chest. My five-year-old body sailed easily to the back of the room. For a few more seconds I rested an eternity. I could hear Bobby yelling at me but he had knocked the wind out of me so I couldn't pay full attention to his words. In the now spinning room I heard his growl through the blinding light. " Wha'da fuck you think yer doin? You think you funny bitch? Wha da fuck game ya think we're playin motherfucker? Get that suit off and get yer ass in the shower NOW!" He raised his right arm and pointed to the adjacent bathroom.

Frantically rushing to get out of the suit I crouched trembling realizing I hadn't taken off

my shoes and they were too large to pull the pants over. I wasn't moving fast enough and I knew it. Rushing forward in one giant step Bobby reminded me with a punch to the top of my head. "Hurry the fuck up, I aint got all night" and I sprawled out on the floor. My brother was still asleep or pretending to be to keep himself out of harm's way.

With a single tremendous yank on my elastic waistband Bobby had not only pulled me off of the ground he also pulled my underwear off by tearing them under my weight. Standing in my socks was good enough for him and he pulled me out of the room and I slid into the bathroom along the cold linoleum.

Two rough, calloused hands lifted me abruptly from the floor and planted me into the half-filled tub. I lost my breath the instant my socked feet hit the freezing cold water. Silently I fought to catch my breath. Though I knew even then that death would not come so easily. Standing there

shivering and breathless in the icy water I didn't realize that Bobby had left the room. Before I knew what was happening I heard my mother screaming from inside the room.

Fully awakened by the cold water I opened my eyes and saw my naked mother slammed onto the toilet just inside the bathroom door. She had come in dragged by her hair wrapped tightly in one of Bobby's giant fists, the other fist firmly wielding a large wooden hairbrush popular in the 1970's. He slapped the backside of the brush against her forehead and began yelling.

"Bitch, you betta shut yo fuckin mouth. I'm not letting this filthy motherfucker in my bed without a bath. You gonna sit here an when we're done you goin to bed too." With that he gave her one more smack with the brush before leaving the room. With blood streaming from her head, my shuddering mother rushed to me and wrapped her arms around me. Her trembling arms made

me tremble even more. I wanted her to get away from me before we were caught.

Luckily, whatever Bobby was doing outside that door was making a lot of noise and we both heard him coming our way. She let go and through chattering teeth said, "I love you. I wish I could help you." I pushed her away as soon as I felt her grip loosen. She sat down on the toilet and mouthed, "I love you" over and over while trying to fight back her tears.

Suddenly the kitchen trashcan appeared in the doorway. Having seen all that I had seen in my five years on earth I shouldn't have been surprised but I was. The dirty trashcan in the little bathroom quickly turned the electrically charged air rancid. As soon as I noticed the bulging bottom of the plastic can the room went dark and ice rained down over my body. It stung and burned my already cold skin. The trashcan covered my body and held buoyant on the water as I sat crying in the now ice-filled tub.

"Get up motherfucker. I didn't tell you to si'down." The can was lifted from the tub. The glaring light made me wince. Bobby's warm, dry hand gripped my neck and yanked me to a standing position. His hand smelled of tobacco, sulfur, and trash. I could only concentrate on the cold still freezing my body. The water in the tub was turning red from the blood dripping from my baby fat skin ripped open by ice. I tried to fold my arms to warm up but my arms were stiff when I tried to bend them and my hands seemed to burn my arm when I touched them. I noticed my chubby arms were turning purple when my mother grabbed me. Pain shot through me like a shock and I screamed in her face. My limbs were becoming frost nipped, I couldn't hold back from the pain. She slapped me hard across the face then began to cry even harder than she already was. I stared at her confused and suddenly alone. Now she and Bobby were attacking me and I had

nowhere to hide, as I stood naked except for my socks in a bathtub full of blood stained ice water. I heard the click of a lighter from the kitchen. A cough and a loud fist on the counter followed. Living with Bobby had sharpened my senses. I had to be aware of everything he was doing at all times when he was in the house. Because not only was I supposed to predict when he would need me so I could be standing in front of him at that moment but knowing where he was and what he was doing was good for my health and safety. So I listened for him at all times, especially times like this. He was getting high in the kitchen but I didn't know what it was he was smoking.

I heard the kitchen faucet running now and he was fumbling around in a manic rage. I knew then I was in trouble. Drawers and doors were slamming every few seconds and the water I was standing in was only getting colder as I lost more and more blood. Debbie was lost in her own pain as she looked at me from the toilet seat. Her knees

were drawn to her chest and her heels balanced her on the toilet. She was as naked and frozen with fear and pain as I was. Her hair was wet and matted against her face in the front but the back stood up in a large hump from having been pulled repeatedly by Bobby before I was woken up.

Bobby liked to hurt Debbie, and hurting me was his favorite way of hurting her. That's all there is too it. Since the day she had met him Bobby owned my mother. Somehow tonight my mother had made Bobby mad and now I was paying the price.

Bobby appeared in the doorway much as he had before. The trashcan was in his arms but this time I knew what to expect. Immediately Debbie began screaming and pulling on Bobby's arm with all of her strength. She was not very strong to begin with. For years Debbie had been addicted to drugs, heroin being her drug of choice. She says she cut back when she was three

months pregnant with me. Once I was out of her she was hooked again. During the six years I lived with her and for years afterward my mother Debbie was a hardcore junkie. Perched on the toilet with glassy red eyes, she began to beg. Bobby liked it when she begged. He made her beg for everything.

"Please not again, please hit me," she screeched in vain.

Without a word Bobby raised his arms, which were again wrapped around the trashcan. Debbie lost her grip. With a flip of his enormous wrists the trashcan rained down ice and water on me. Gasping for breath my mouth filled with trashy iced water and I began to choke. The water and ice combination drenched my nearly frozen body and burned like fire pouring over me. The water dulled the ice but it pelted the already open cuts and stung like needles through the fire. Engulfed in pain and suffocating I fell to my knees into the ice water. Bobby seized the moment as if it had

197

been choreographed. Without turning around he threw the trashcan behind him and out the door. It hit the hallway wall and was then reflected toward the kitchen. Cowering on the toilet Debbie tucked her knees closer to her face and wrapped her arms around them as a shield against the airborne trashcan.

I was still in the middle of a cough to clear my throat when Bobby's enormous hand covered the back of my head. My faced slammed into the ice water forcing more water into my throat. Panic was immediate and my frozen limbs began to flail. Bobby pulled me out of the water and planted a piercing elbow into my back. The force of the elbow blow had me nearly bent in half backward in the tub. He put his face against mine. His breath was disgusting, metallic and hot. "Boy, you aint gonna die so quick ya son of a bitch. I got plans for you tonight. Ain'dat right bitch?" Bobby said as he turned around to face my mother.

Debbie whimpered but did not move.

With my soaking wet hair in his left hand he reached up to the sink and grabbed the brush again with his right. The brush cracked against the top of Debbie's head over and over. "Answer me bitch!"

Crack!

"We gonna have some fun"

Crack!

"Aint we?"

Crack!

He shoved the words from his mouth as he pounded the brush against my mother's head. He was nearly breathless now from all of the activity. I could hear his heart hammering as he leaned in close to me. He must have been burning speed in the kitchen. His ashy brown skin was aglow with sweat and excitement. Again he forced me under the water.

My face was smashed against the bottom of the tub. My shoulders wedged there also, my feet flew

into the air. Anchored like a tripod beneath the water I grabbed for Bobby's wrist with both hands. Frantic and cold, I hyperventilated and swallowed more water. My hands and feet flew in all directions trying to get from under the weight on the back of my head. Lifeless, my legs collapsed into the water. I had no more fight left in me and I went limp. For a few seconds I felt no pain but instead felt comfort and calm.

The icy water settled Bobby's mania. He pulled my head from the water and held my face to his. He wasn't sweating any more and he looked relaxed, and sinister.

Smiling he said, "Dry y'ass off, now!"

He draped me over the side of the tub with a force that evacuated blood and water from my mouth to the floor.

I didn't watch as Bobby dragged my mother from the bathroom. I was told to dry off and that's what I did. Though I knew something else was about to happen it felt good to be alone and dry.

Even if the towel felt like sandpaper on my body it was much warmer out of the tub than in it. The towel was navigated gently around each of the cuts I could see. Tending to my own wounds had become common and I was gentle with myself. Upon inspection my skin was ripped, purple, and more fragile than usual. I felt no pity for my situation but as I stood there I wished for death. Every night and every day I hoped that that day would bring my death. I knew that death would be the only escape from the torture and pain. My dissociation to the grave was hastily discontinued by Bobby's hulking frame entering the bathroom. Reaching out with a massive hand aimed at my throat, Bobby was the most terrifying thing I had ever seen. At that moment I was seeing him for the first time. At that moment I was looking at a new man, a more vicious and volatile creature than the one I had lived with for the last several years.

Excitedly he said, "Le's go mufucka. I got somethin for you."

Wrenching me off the floor, Bobby flung my body around effortlessly. My head smacked the doorframe as he heaved me into the hall. My bedroom door was closed, and there was no light coming from underneath. Behind that door Matthew was sound asleep.

The sheets were torn off of their bed at each corner and bunched up beneath my mother who was curled up on her side in the center of it all. Freeing my neck from his hand, Bobby heaved me onto the bed. Debbie scuttled the few inches to me and huddled her body on top of mine for protection. Something hit her on the back and the force reverberated through my body.

"Get off that mufucka," he warned.

His massive chest heaved as he took a deep breath and continued, "Aint no use, bitch. You got it comin."

The brush appeared in the big man's hand and he hammered it across her head. She let loose her embrace to shield her head from subsequent blows. Bobby grabbed my shins and tore me from my mother's cover. Heaped onto the floor at the foot of the bed I stared up at Bobby. He pulled my mother's legs taut. Her feet appeared in my face. They looked strikingly pink against his hard brown skin. His hands wrapped easily around her ankles, his forearms bulged from the effort of dragging her into position. When her knees and back were flat against the bed he crawled on top of her in a position I had seen many times. I thought I would be watching them have sex again. He called it "havin his old lady". Instead of mounting her, he crawled over her. His crotch was on her face. This too I had seen many times but this time his clothes were on and he was reaching for the nightstand next to the bed. He opened the drawer with his right hand and fumbled around in the drawer. Pulling out several

things he saved some on the bed, others he tossed aside onto the carpet. His left hand was sorting through those things he placed on the bed. Over his arched back I watched him stuff something under a pillow that had been crammed between the bare wall and the mattress.

Bobby rolled off of the bed. Undoing his belt he walked to the door and flipped the switch on the light. He moved the few steps back to the bed and turned on the light that stood on the nightstand. Long ago a red scarf had been thrown over the top of the lamp so the room was instantly bathed in red light. I was still lumped on the floor while Bobby manipulated my mother's prostrate limbs. This was all too familiar and now I knew I would be watching Bobby "have his old lady."

"Put'yer face in it!" demanded the beast I had met in the bathroom.

He pointed to my mother's pubic hair. I knew more about sex then than I should have. Bobby had made me watch him rape my mother many

times. I knew that I did not want to put my face down there.

"Motherfucker" he snarled.

Then his teeth clenched tightly, "I said put yo face in it and I mean put yo gotdamn face in'at shit NOW!" The words narrowly escaped his mouth.

Debbie started to raise herself off of the bed in objection. Bobby reached behind his back and whipped his right hand over his head and came down on Debbie's head with such force that it sounded like two rocks colliding. From his clenched fist his gun appeared. It was small and black with a brown handle. It was a gun I had seen often. Bobby liked to wield it when we broke into houses. He wore it in his sock when we went around the corner. He almost never left the house without it.

He put the gun in his left hand and cleared the bloody hair from my mother's face with his right. The hair was caked and matted from the dried

blood and random hairs still clung to her face as if they too wanted to escape Bobby's grasp. The long red hairs looked like scars across Debbie's stark white face. Bobby tightened his grip on the hair still in his hand.

"Tell that little mufucka to do it or I'm aunna fuckin do it and you don' want me da fuckin do it."

I could hardly make out what she was saying through the tears and then she stammered out, "B,b,b,baby, do as your daddy tells you." She sucked in her snot and tears with a loud snort and continued, "Please do as your daddy tells you." He wasn't my daddy but he liked to be called that, especially when he was beating me. Also, I wasn't defying him or attempting to not do as I was told. I was in shock and I was frozen in place. I didn't want to know what was going to happen. I did not want to put my face near my mother. My body, scorched from the ice bath, could not move from the floor.

Through his clenched teeth came the staggered instruction, "Open yo fuckin mouf. Do it. Open yo fuckin mouf, now!"

My lips parted and the grimy gun barrel slammed into my mouth. The steel crashed against my teeth as my tongue pressed into the opening of the barrel. Bobby's finger was on the trigger as he cocked the hammer down.

"Suck it mufucka, suck that shit down." His spit stung my face as he barked the order.

Turning to Debbie writhing on the bed, he sneered, "You like that, bitch? You better tell this sonuvabitch to do as he's told or he aint gonn' be alive no more." He pounded his fist into her face and she was instantly still.

Lying prone on the bed I heard her shriek, "Please baby, do it, just do as your told. Please baby. Pleeease!" Her last word came out as she choked again on her tears.

She pled as if I had a choice. I had been beaten raw in the deepest part of the night. I was

exhausted and weak. Disobedience was not my goal. I sucked the gun barrel as if it were candy I was seldom afforded.

"You look just like your whore mother, you faggot. You suck it so good maybe you should be suckin my dick and teach her somethin."

He turned his glaring eyes to Debbie, "What you think about that bitch? You want our boy to show you how to suck a man's dick?"

It was more a threat than a question.

He turned back and watched me intently and I could see his forearms sweating again as he slowly slid the gun back and forth over my lips.

As I noticed his erection he quickly pulled the gun out of my mouth and set the weapon on the dresser that stood behind me. He bent over the slightest bit putting his head near the top of the dresser. Placing a length of a straw in his nose he snorted something from the mirror that I knew was up there. His head roared back while the straw was dropped back to the mirror. He

squeezed his nose closed with one hand and spit on the carpet. I wiped the saliva from my mouth trying to get rid of the powdery taste of the gun. Then the gun was waving between my face and my mother's crotch while he said again, "Put'yer face in it."

I pushed myself to my feet and flopped my head on my mother's soft belly. My face stuck to her sweating torso immediately. My skin screamed as Bobby's powerful hand peeled me from her warmth and he jerked me into position. Thrown between Debbie's legs, my arms bent beneath my bony chest as my shoulders were pinned against her thighs. My nose burned as I stared between my mother's legs.

Bobby gripped the back of my head and hissed, "Lick it boy."

She stunk of filth, sweat and urine. I obeyed.

"Yeah, mufucka. That's my boy," he gloated.

As he waved the gun back and forth I trained my stare on Bobby as I obeyed. My body was

comfortable and warm. Looking at Debbie he stammered out,

"*Sprea'dat shit bitch.* Let the boy *in.*" His voice was cool and he was high.

The tone of his voice told me that this was only the beginning. Bobby's rage was wild and unpredictable, but once it began subtle cues clearly delineated a cycle. He was only now catching his stride. It was going to be a long night.

Debbie's fingernails gouged my flesh as her hands appeared in my face. She was still scratching my face when she pushed my head backward and out of her way. Her knuckles were clammy against my cheek. Smoothing back the pubic hair shot its putrid odor directly into my nose. She splayed her fingers and pressed her palms to the inside of her thighs. Bobby's voice broke in, exacerbating my horror.

"Yeah girl. You know how da do it," he said, smooth talking his old lady.

His head dipped forward to punctuate the words that slurred toward me excitedly, "Now get on *'nat shit* boy. Lick *that* shit. 'At's good shit."

He stepped quickly behind me, snorted the powder from the dresser, and stepped back beside me with the gun pressed against the back of my head. It was no longer cocked but his finger remained perched on the hammer.

"Lick it boy. Lick that pussy. She like to have her pussy out and damn sure I aint eatin'at shit. You gonn' b'eating *dat shit all night,*" he said while licking white powder from the tips of his fingers, "till I tell you ta stop. And when you done, you gonn' keep goin'. Ya hear me boy?" His ghastly voice forced the question through clenched teeth. I cowered in response.

I didn't dare say anything. He didn't ever want to hear my voice. Years before, Bobby had taught me the rules to taking a beating and he corrected my mistakes with more beatings. The rules to taking a beating: stand up, stand still, hands to the

sides, never say a word unless told to speak, crying makes it worse.

Debbie cried and squirmed as my mouth awkwardly maneuvered around her most intimate region. The smell wasn't as bad anymore but my nose continued to burn as I followed Bobby's instructions. Bobby had no patience. He liked to give orders and they were to be followed exactly as he wanted, the first time. It was best not to hesitate and questioning was never an option. While I chose to concentrate on Debbie's crying to occupy my mind it had seemed to escape Bobby's attention until now. Feeling the release of pressure on the back of my head I looked up to see Bobby flip the gun on his finger and smash the butt of the gun into my mother's forehead and begin to yell.

"Bitch you *know* you like it. You don't stop crying I'm gonn' make *this* little mufucka cry." He pushed the gun from her face to mine and back

again. "Which it gonn' be bitch?" he asked, holding the butt of the gun inches from her face. She sucked her lips trying to hold in her cries. Satisfied by her stifled whimper, Bobby turned his eyes to me. To avoid a thunderous blast from the butt of the gun, I stuck my tongue out and continued as before.

"Oh yeah boy, you likin'at shit aint ya?" he roared on the verge of laughter.

"Bitch, this boy gonn' be after that shit all the time now baby. We gonn' have a lot of fun wit' dis mufucka now." He sneered, waving his head with a wicked grin.

"I aint gonn' be able t'do *my* business with this little fucker eatin all his momma all day." Bobby was enthusiastic and impressing himself when my mother let out a sharp, piercing scream. I thought my mother had just died with my head trapped between her legs. Her chest convulsed and she began to breath heavily after Bobby suddenly fell

another blow with the butt of the gun to her forehead. She was still alive.

"Shut yo mouf bitch." He warned as his head cocked to the side.

Suddenly the taste changed. I pulled away. Bobby noticed my reaction, and smiled.

"Get up" he said while abruptly hoisting me onto my feet.

"Bitch look at'is boy's dick," he ordered while pointing the gun at my five-year old penis.

"How the hell he gonna be fuckin you if you aint got no dick hard. What tha fuck's yo problem? That boy done gone and made you come and you can't even get him hard? Bitch you a sorry piece'a ass." He bent down slowly and wrapped a giant fist in her matted hair, pulling her upper body off of the bed. He swung the gun to her face and then at me.

"Suck his dick," he casually commanded.

"Suck 'at little dick," he repeated as he began to sweat.

"You better get that little mufucka hard and if you stop before it's hard…" He wasn't done when Debbie suddenly came to life and clawed at Bobby's face throwing her legs in the air trying to get away from his grasp.

"Nooohohohoh!" Her chest heaved as she pushed out her plea.

Her legs flailed around until she got her feet under her. Feet planted, she raised her body from the bed. Her hair still encased in Bobby's fist, she was naked and bent over backward standing on the bed. Bobby's other fist, still holding the gun, landed a crushing blow to her arched mid-section. His punch robbed Debbie of her momentum and she splashed, defeated, onto the bed. He jerked his hand loose from her hair and spit on her face before he jammed the grimy gun barrel between her eyes.

"Gettin'at dick in ya mouf get y'all excited bitch?" He goaded while he caught his breath.

The drugs had stolen his stamina but that only made him work harder and grow more agitated and angry. He punched her in the face. When she opened her mouth to cry he jammed four fingers of his left hand into her mouth and gripped her chin with his thumb. With her jaw in his grip he ripped her head from the bed. Sitting her up straight on the rumpled bed he slapped each side of her face with the backside of his right hand that still gripped the snub nose .38.

He shook his head and roared, "You never fuckin learn," as he leaned his weight forward and rapped her in the face with the gun again. His left hand still held her mouth open and her head up. Her head unable to recoil from the shock, her face absorbed the full intensity of the blow. The butt of the gun split her face open below her eye. The blood raced down her cheek and pooled with her tears in Bobby's palm.

"I tol' ya ya better learn from this boy. Now don' say a gotdamn word. N'don' think of fuckin'

wit'me again," he yelled as he pounded his fist
into her face again.

Bobby stared at Debbie and growled while
flipping the gun back into position pointing at my
penis, "Now you fuckin move or I'ma shoot this
mufucka's dick *off!*"

He turned and ripped me from the floor and
stood me on the bed next to my bleeding mother.
He grabbed my penis between two of his giant
calloused knuckles. He jerked my body toward
Debbie.

With a slap that rocked her body backward he
demanded, "Take this mufucka's dick in ya mouf
and get it hard."

He swung his arm and jammed the gun between
her legs where my face had just been and asked,
"Or'm I gonn have to kill him and fuck you wit'
my piece?"

The words hung in the air, and I waited for her to
do something. Bobby gave me a last tug that flung
me against my mother.

217

Bobby reached down and cleared Debbie's hair from her face. He pulled the crusty hair from her forehead and cheeks. She whimpered and squealed from the pain. When Bobby could see clearly that Debbie was doing as she was told, he laughed and slapped my bare backside. My skin had only just begun to warm up and was cut all over. His slap sent a tearing pain straight through me. Debbie bit my penis as my body slammed into her face. I grunted the pain away with my mouth closed tightly. Bobby backed off to take another snort from the dresser. His hands fumbled around the dresser top, he picked something up and then stepped in close to the bed. He stroked Debbie's head lovingly from her forehead back. When his hand reached the top of her neck he pushed her head against my body. I stood on the bed still holding my hands on Debbie's shoulders. She was warm and sweaty. The heat felt good against my body sore from the barrage of pain. I didn't completely understand

what was happening. I had watched Debbie do this to Bobby and many other different men and I knew what it had done to them. I wondered if I was supposed to like it too.

Stepping back to survey his victory, Bobby put a joint in his mouth and through pursed lips cooed, "Yeah baby, ya got that little piece'a dick in ya mouf like ya mean it," he paused to light the reefer.

"That's all I want baby," he said while inhaling a huge drag to keep his joint lit.

"Ya do as ya told," he coughed, "and it'll be alright." His voice cut through the air now thickening with smoke.

Bobby sat down in a chair against the wall behind me. He reclined as he smoked his joint. The air was heavy with smoke and while I rested against Debbie's head I felt a strange sensation in my penis. Nearly simultaneously Debbie pulled her head back away from my body and began to gasp for air.

"Ho − lee shit!" Bobby said with a chuckle. "Ya got that damn thing hard like I knew ya would," he congratulated her.

Debbie wiped her mouth while I stood between her legs on the bed. Poking out at Debbie's face was my penis. It was pointed straight into the air. I had never seen it look that way before, and it was bigger than I'd ever seen. My tiny erection was very exciting to Bobby who rushed from his chair to see. As he approached the bed, he held out his hand that held the lit joint.

"Ya wan' hit this shit?" he asked while holding the joint out to Debbie with a smile. She reached for it, and he pulled it away. He put it to her lips and let her drag. Bobby liked to accent his cruelty with a fleeting show of kindness. She leaned her head back to blow out the smoke after several hits. He grabbed her dangling hair and swung her body around so her head was facing the top of the bed. She jutted her arms out and scurried on her

hands to avoid being entirely dragged. She bent her legs and crawled away from me like a crab.

"Now is for real, bitch. Show me. Show ME how you gonn' fuck. Now, you love dis mufucka so much you gonn' fuck him right here'n now, come on bitch."

Debbie choked and began to cry but before the first tear came the gun reappeared, the hammer cocked back and the room went silent.

"You done all that work now you gone finish it." He picked me up as I stared at my two-inch erection. He placed me gently on top of my mother, my face between her breasts. I turned my head to the side and closed my eyes ready to fall asleep. My eyes reopened quickly when the rough palm of Bobby's hand cradled my head while his strong stiff fingers raked through my hair and ripped me from rest.

"You're gonn' do as I tell you or I'ma fuckin' kill you, you un'stand me mufucka?"

Turning my eyes from his I tried to maneuver my tired, aching body into the position I had seen so many men take on top of my mother.

My hands sank into her soft, hollow torso as I tried to raise my body. Reaching down for my mother's hips I trusted that she would not let this happen. Debbie's arms were snaking their way toward me as my eyes begged her to make it stop. Her bony arm locked and lifted my chest from hers while her fingers, like tendrils, wrapped themselves around my penis. Her quivering hand jerked my penis back and forth. Her head twitching violently, she was never able to fully touch her lips to my face as she leaned down to kiss me. Through spit and tears she whispered, "I'm sorry…" then her lips disappeared inside her mouth.

My back was sagging from my weight and exhaustion. My hands pressed painfully onto Debbie's stabbing hipbones. As I entered her, she placed her hand firmly on my backside and

pushed my body into hers. Our bodies were connected, and I started to cry.

Suddenly the room was ablaze with light, and a blistering snap cracked through the smoke filled room. In Bobby's menacing grasp was the red bandana from atop the lamp. Through squinted eyes I watched him flip his mighty wrist. Then the bandana whipped across my face, stinging the dried cuts and tearing them open once more.

"What the fuck you cryin for boy?" The words choked out of his mouth as he held in the smoke from his joint.

"Boy you losin that cherry wit my favorite bitch," was all he had to say before he slapped me again. Debbie's pubic bone jammed into my belly and I was nearly thrust off of her, but Bobby's hand forced me back into her. After several gut-wrenching thrusts and head slaps, I recognized the rhythm and fell into step with her. Debbie's face was discolored and sunken like the dead woman's I had seen several weeks earlier. She

made no sound, but I could see her chest heave as she breathed laboriously.

Bobby continued hitting my head but gradually eased the intensity until he was only slapping out Debbie's rhythm as if it were a drum. He was standing beside me, hitting me with his right hand on the back of my head. He held his joint firmly in his left. He was stoned, but he dragged on his joint until it burned his fingers and lips. In the heavy gray air, Bobby knocked me off of Debbie and slid himself into position on top of her and began tenderly kissing her face.

His kisses fell sloppily across her torn, bruised face. She cried silently while his body slithered atop her paralyzed frame. His leathery hands groped her battered skin. Carelessly his giant palms molded her bloodstained face, stretching the flesh apart where the butt of the gun had cut her. His fingers ripped through her matted scarlet hair, pinning her head to the bed.

"Oh… baby… I… love… you…" He said, half paying attention. His head nodded back and forth as he held her head firmly to the bed. Debbie offered no resistance to the mauling. Bobby's backhand had sent me to the floor on the right side of the bed, where I was an insensible heap. "Baby, baby, baby, ya know why I love you? Cause you do what you tol' and you aint no bullshit," he whispered with his head swaying. "Where dat fuckin boy? Mufucka get up hea'. You gon' see how a real mufucka do dis shit. Right baby?" The snap and unzip of his pants rang in my ears as he gave the order. I pushed myself from the floor in time to see Bobby pulling his pants down over his backside, his filthy white underwear peeling off his skin and snapping inside the pants.

"Pull deez pants off me boy," he demanded as my head appeared at the side of the bed. Holding tightly to the mattress, I hoisted myself from the floor and traveled around the side of the bed.

Bobby's feet were soon in my face. I released the mattress and grabbed for the pant legs hanging off the bed. Stepping back I tugged at the crusted blue jeans. Exhaustion made my hands burn as I gripped the fabric. Leaning backward the pants slowly came free from his ashy legs. My back clumsily smashed into the chest of drawers. "Get'yer ass up her boy. You gon' watch me give it'ta ya mama so ya do it right next time," he growled looking back at me still holding her head to the bed.

"Shut up bitch," he yelled as Debbie began to whimper. He bounced her head on the bed as he rocked his shoulders forward. I pushed myself from the dresser to the bed and carefully climbed onto the foot of the bed while trying to position myself as far away from Bobby as I could. He reached back with his right hand and got a hold of my hair and smashed my face into my mother's hipbone, "Watch ri'there mufucka and don' move!" he ordered. My head rested against my

mother's hip and I watched as Bobby jammed his erect penis inside my mother as she squealed and began to cry again.

Over and over he thrust his penis into her. When her cries became louder he pounded his fist into her face and commanded, "Bitch, you better be cryin outta joy, tell me how good dis feel or I'ma hit ya'gain!" He was yelling, but he never lost his rhythm not even when he hit her.

She complied through the tears, "You're so big it hurts baby, that's why I'm cryin, you know I love it. Please don't stop." Her bloody, fat lips quivered as they released the words. He pushed her head into the bed with one hand and my head closer to his penis as he suddenly stopped moving. He collapsed on top of my mother with my head stuck between their bodies. Neither of them moved to let me free.

The smell was musky and strong, and I tried to pull my head loose. Bobby's weight was too much for my tiny body, and I remained stuck. I held my

breath to avoid the smell. As my mouth forced itself open to breathe, Bobby rolled to his left and away from my head and Debbie's body. I thought we were free. When I had watched them have sex before I was always allowed to leave when Bobby rolled off of her. Thinking it was over I waited to be dismissed.

"Come here you little sonuvabitch," he said playfully as he grabbed me under my armpit and pulled toward him. He was at the head of the bed, lying comfortably with his head resting on a stack of pillows. He pulled me to him, flipped me over and tucked me into the curve his massive chest with his left arm holding me firmly against him. Debbie had somehow gotten herself on his opposite side in nearly the same position.

"Ya know I loves yer momma. And I woke ya up to tell ya that I love ya momma so much I been wantin us to be a family," his words were soft and slow.

"Ya momma don't always believe me when I tell her I loves her but I know you know. Doncha boy?" it wasn't a question. He continued, "Reach on over inta that draw and get that big box fa' me," he said. He relaxed his forearm and popped his bicep, which propelled me into a seated position. I leant to my left toward the nightstand and opened the drawer. I pulled out the box that I had held so many times. They kept their drugs in the box, and I was regularly sent to fetch it from the other room. I handed the box to Bobby. Thinking I need to cook some dope I started to get up to get his lighter that I could clearly see on the other side of the room.

"Where you goin' boy? I got what you want right here, get back over here."

He pulled me back toward him and placed the box on his belly. I lay there confused, trying not to breathe, waiting for the blow that didn't come. His body odor was strong and frightening, his

sweat burning the cuts along the right side of my
body.

"I'm aunna marry ya mother boy and I'm gon'
be ya daddy from now on," he said. From the box
on his belly, he pulled a smaller black box,
placing it in front of me.

"Open it. That's what I woke ya ass up fo'," he
commanded, shaking his head at my ignorance.
The box was hard but covered in a soft velvety
fabric. It felt good in my hand, and I didn't want
to let go. When I tried to open it, I didn't have
the strength. Frustrated, Bobby grabbed the box
from my hand.

"Ya dumb mufucka can't do shit." He opened the
box. "Look at *that* mufucka. Dat's ya mom's
weddin' ring. We gettin' married someday, and
you and Matt gon' be mine just like ya momma
is." He pushed the box closer to my face.

"When you wanna get married baby?" he cooed
at my mother.

"Any time you want baby. I can't wait till we're married, and I can wear that ring. It's beautiful."

"Come on now, get up. I gotta piss." He kissed Debbie's head and pushed me to the floor.

"Put dat shit away and getcha ass to bed. And don' let me catch ya fuckin 'round witchya brother neither." Nearly stepping on me as he got out of bed, I heard him using the toilet before I was off the floor.

I crept back to the room I shared with Matthew and snuck into the bed. He was sprawled across the bed, but I was still small enough to lie at the other end without unsettling him. Awake and in pain, I wished that this were all a dream. I wanted my whole life to be the dream of an infant, hoping that any minute I would awaken as a newborn child in the hospital nursery. This couldn't be my life; this couldn't be anyone's real life.

Chapter Eleven
Fight or Flight

When the kids act up in class, we just deal with it.
I have a special relationship with my kids and
their families, and to do this work, we all have to
know and trust each other. I make a concerted
effort to know each of my students and their
families, and thus gain their trust. However, when
my kids get out of control or make poor decisions
outside of my classroom, the consequences are
beyond my control. Such a situation occurred one
afternoon, and the student was lucky not to have
been arrested, which would have broken my
heart.

Jack was a strong, athletic young man. He was
very intelligent, but frequently refused to show it.
If I were to ever mention it out loud, he would
explode in anger as if I had insulted him. He had
a reputation to uphold, and in his world, being
smart was equal to being soft. He had had a very
hard life coming up. From the day he was

abandoned in the street as a newborn until the day he found himself in my class, he had struggled and fought for everything he had and every breath he took. He was a survivor in every sense of the word. I identified with his spirit and resilience.

Teachers are not supposed to have favorites, but Jack was my favorite in his class. In casual conversation about the year's class, I told my principal that Jack would be my toughest challenge of the year, but if he were to make it to the end he would also be my biggest success. And I meant it.

Early in the school year, Jack was called to the office to see his guidance counselor at 11:30. He wasn't gone long, but when he returned he had a letter in his hand and a scowl on his face. I assumed it was a letter from his father. Since the beginning of the school year, he had been writing to his father who was incarcerated in another state.

"What's wrong little brother?" I asked trying to break the mood.

"Damn office opened my fuckin letter," he blurted out, as he shook his head like a bull ready to charge.

"Sir, please don't use profanity in class." I said.

"I'm sorry Mr. Love, but I'm pissed off. They had no right to open my f'n letter." He continued, as he slammed his tense body into his chair.

"Sir, how do you know that someone in the office opened it? Did they tell you they opened it, or do you think they opened it?" I asked quickly.

He jumped into an acrobatic tirade, speaking frankly of his dislike and distrust of the school and its staff. As they had all been taught to do, the rest of the class continued on with their work while Jack and I spoke. When I attempted to continue on with class and asked the boys to work on their science, we all noticed that another student had fallen asleep during the commotion. Jack

immediately became verbally abusive of the student.

Jack, like so many students, would throw a tantrum and take up everyone's time without a single thought about the other students or the work they may be trying to complete. However, unlike most any student I've ever had, Jack could throw a tantrum, exhaust himself, then sit down and complete the work he should have been doing in the first place. He would even complete it with greater accuracy and in less time than most anyone else as well. With the student asleep, everyone knew that our time was wasting away. When students disrupt the class, including falling asleep, that time must be made up by the class in order to get the day's work completed. Jack's only thought was of having to make up this time by missing his free time in the gym. When I tried to redirect him and remind him that he already owed me his time for his previous outburst, his rage switched from the other student

to personal attacks on my assistant and me. He used profanity-laced tirades to describe the atmosphere of the class, our personal lives, and how poorly we treat him. I cocked my head toward the door, which my assistant understood was our signal to escort the rest of the class out. Jack's frustration went on for nearly an hour. When I told him that he was getting too excited and agitated about the letter issue and that I was sure I could help him get to the bottom of it, he began to cuss again, and said he did not care about the letter. Then he pulled it from his pocket, ripped it up, and threw it away. I knew there was no turning back for him now. I had pulled a similar move with a letter from Debbie when I was a few years younger than Jack.

He began to wander the room in a frenzy. He was picking things from my desk, the podium and other places out of his assigned area. He began to threaten to kill teachers in the school who, he said, had him locked up. He then threatened to

kill both my assistant and me, in addition to blowing up the school. In a typical school setting, this type of behavior would be grounds for expulsion. However, in an Alternative setting this behavior is dealt with on a more individual basis. I approached Jack from across the room and pulled a student desk toward him, sitting him in it. Then I placed one hand on the back of his chair and one hand on the desktop, blocking him in the chair. He told me to get away from him and again became verbally abusive.

I stood at his desk for just over twenty minutes, speaking with him about his father, his feelings, and his warranted anger. I also discussed other ways he could have dealt with his anger. He spoke with me calmly, and we had a very mature conversation. Going back to the cause of his outburst, I asked him if he really believed that the office staff had opened his letter, since they had never opened any of our letters before. Immediately he clammed up and made a sudden

move to get up from the seat. I blocked his exit, and he was forced back into the seat. He began to swing at me in wild, frantic motions, as he struggled to get out of the seat. He thrashed violently and got to his feet. Once out of the confines of the student desk I was able to restrain him, though he continued to threaten me. He told me that when he got free he was going to spit in my mouth, among other things. I told him that I would let him loose as soon as he settled down, and then I quit talking.

He calmed quickly, used to the routine. I let him free, and he sat quietly for a few moments. He apologized for threatening me.

"Mr. Love, I didn't mean nothin' against you." He said tranquilly as he sat cross-legged on the mat we were sitting on. I could see his anger rising on his face, as he spoke about his father's letter. Without warning, he darted to his feet. He pushed some electronic equipment from a classroom media cart that was close by. Running

across the room, he stood with his back to a corner and threw a desk across the front of the room, knocking over several other desks. As I strode toward him, he grabbed his book bag and headed out the door. This all took place in a matter of seconds.

I followed Jack outside of the room, where I saw a guidance counselor. My assistant had alerted her. I asked the counselor to contact the school's on-staff police officer, known as an SRO, as I followed Jack out of the building. The SRO is a School Resource Officer, a sheriff's deputy assigned to the school. Most schools have at least one as part of the staff. I followed Jack for several hundred feet to a stop sign by the front of the school. Pausing briefly, he turned to look at me. Hesitantly he continued to walk down the road with me behind him. He knocked over three or four mailboxes along the roadside, which I tried to place back upright as I walked by. Calling behind him, I finally convinced him to stop, and

he spoke with me briefly as I approached. The SRO and my principal arrived simultaneously upon the scene. We all spoke with Jack quickly until he agreed to return to the school. The SRO walked back to the building with Jack, and I drove back with the principal, detailing the incident as we drove.

Once back at school, the four of us met in the principal's office. After some discussion and reassurances from the principal that no one had opened his letter, but that it had come through the mail that way, Jack relaxed, but remained silent. To my chagrin, it was determined that we had no other recourse than to suspend Jack for several days. He remained calm and silent until his grandmother came to pick him up. I walked to my room, defeated and sad that I was not able to help Jack work through his anger. I knew it was not my place or responsibility to correct the evils and tragedies in the lives of my students, but having felt their anger and disappointment so

often myself at their age, I wanted so desperately to wipe it all away for each of them.

Arriving back at my classroom, I dutifully went on with teaching, and the day ended without incident or much mention of the previous incident. We had a short discussion on conflict resolution and class rules, and the boys were all very cooperative and understanding. My students left for the day, but my disquiet lingered. An idea came to me, and without a second thought, I sat down at my desk and penned a letter to Jack's father. In the letter, I did my best to describe Jack's reaction to the unsealed envelope without too much emotion. I focused the letter on Jack as a whole person and tried to tell the man as many positive details about Jack's school experience as I could. When the letter was completed it was several pages long. To complement the letter, I enclosed an unofficial copy of Jack's current grades, which were excellent, and a Polaroid picture of Jack I had taken several days earlier.

Feeling much better, I left school and headed to the post office.

Earlier in the term, Jack had asked if we could read <u>Handbook for Boys</u> by Walter Dean Myers. I had previously owned a copy but had, at some point, given it away. I ordered a classroom set of about ten copies, and during the time Jack was suspended, they arrived. Having never been to his home, I decided it was a good time to check on him. At the end of the school day, I stacked a small collection of textbooks and an inscribed copy of <u>Handbook for Boys</u> together and headed to Jack's house across town.

I had been warned about Jack's neighborhood as being one of the roughest in town. While I wasn't worried, I did find the warnings very humorous. People's assumptions always entertain me. With the top of my Jeep down, I drove over to Jack's house. I drove slowly through his neighborhood of small, single-story concrete row houses. This is what passed for "projects" in the south, and the

stark contrast to my own experiences made me laugh to myself as I thought of everyone's warnings. Cat calls and invitations of "Hey White Boy, come on over here," rang through the streets from the disparate groups of porch dwellers. I knew they were meant for me, as I was the only "white" person in sight.

Finding the house, I stepped from the Jeep and walked confidently toward the small brick duplex. A voice from behind me yelled, "Hey! Hey! What you doin' there? That's my house! What you want?" I turned and waved, as it was really much too far to yell a true explanation in response. Before I got to the front step, Jack burst through the screen door wearing a tank top and sagging denim shorts.

He yelled across the street, "Yo! This is my teacher. Ya'll mess with him I'ma kick yo ass!" His voice was loud, strong, and sincere. I smiled at him and put out my hand. He shook it with vigor.

"Mr. Love, Sir, what you doin' here?" He asked pleasantly.

"I brought you some things that you might need while you're out, as well as something you've been wanting." I said as I handed him the stack of books.

He looked down past the pile of familiar textbooks and zeroed in on the little paperback novel sitting on top. "Oh, Mr. Love, where did you find this?" He asked as he held the paperback up and flipped through it as if fanning a stack of cash. He balanced the hulking stack of textbooks against his torso. His excitement was contagious. "It was with your stuff. I figured it was yours, so I brought it to you." I said, trying to sound sincere.

"Sir, you know this aint mine. You wrote in it," he said, noticing the inscription on the inside front cover. He put the stack of textbooks on the porch and held the novel open as if it were a sacred relic. His mouth moved, as he read through the inscription. I saw his mouth widen

into a smile, but it quickly faded as he looked up at my face. "I don't deserve this." He said emphatically.

"Yes Sir, you do." I answered.

"Sir, I was a jerk to you and everyone else. Now you giving me this book with all these good things you wrote inside. I don't deserve this, Sir."

"Sir, we all deserve a lot more than we get, but we take what we get and we deal with it. Good and bad. You're a great student and what better gift than your own copy of <u>Handbook for Boys</u>. To be honest though, everyone in class got one, I just didn't write in theirs." I said with a reassuring smile.

"Mr. Love, why you so nice to me?" He asked, still holding the book in front of him.

"Because you remind me of myself. All of you do. I love you like I love every student I ever had or will have. You just think I'm only nice to you because you don't see me with everyone else. I hate to break it to you, but I'm good to all of my

kids. You need teachers like me so you know that there are adults, especially teachers, that you can trust and respect."

"I don't get you, Sir." He said in response.

"Me either." I said, nodding my head with a cheerful smile, "I'm gonna get out of here and head back to school. I'll see you in a few days. There are lesson plans in your textbooks. Make sure you get that work done!"

"Yes Sir," he said, as he bent to pick up his books and returned to the dark inside of his house. As I drove away from his neighborhood, there were no calls or insults or propositions. It was as if word had spread that I was there for a legitimate reason and was allowed to pass unfettered. It was comforting to see Jack and know that he was not angry. It was exciting to see Jack excited at having a book of his own, a book that he had wanted. A few days later, Jack was back at school. Soon afterwards, I received a letter from Jack's father. I was shocked by the immediacy of his

response. I was shocked to get a response at all. Hiding the letter was difficult as I wanted to read it, but I had no privacy in the classroom. I didn't want Jack to know until I had read it, and even then I wasn't sure if I'd tell him. When the class cleared out for the day, I sat at my desk and opened the letter. It read as follows (some changes were made to disguise the identity of the child):

Mr. Love,

I would like to start out by saying "Thank You" for the letter and the progress report that you sent me. I appreciate the time and effort that you are sharing with your kids and especially mine, "Jack". I understand everything that Jack is going through at this time. I believe you are the best teacher for him at this time. Jack needs a lot of encouragement and guidance because he can be a real great kid at times. I believe that the places were he is living (Projects) and the negative

environment can be an unhealthy place for him. That's why when I get out in 10 months I will be fighting for the both of us to make our lives better! I was born and raised in that town. I went to your school. I remember Mrs. Roberts my reading teacher telling my mother that she didn't understand what was wrong with me. I had a behavioral problem in school too. You might have made a profound affect in my life, if we had a teacher teaching Alternative/Behavioral classes for kids back then. I plan to make myself very active in his life and help him and encourage him to get his schooling because if I had been wiser back then I would have chosen the Right Path of life, considering how a life of crime has made mine so miserable. I love Jack and I don't want to see him following in my footsteps. How long is Jack going to be in the Alternative/Behavioral classes.

I was really surprised when I first start getting letters from Jack because I could tell he

was angry with me for being locked up. Jack was living up with me and when I had sent him back, that's when he had start being rebellious and was sent off from his grandmother.

I only hope that he is not doing any of the things that he is saying he's doing? I believe his first letter was to get me upset because that's exactly what he had done because I stayed up in my bed until 4:00 am thinking about him. I was kind of confused at first because the letters was coming from the school.

I believe writing these letters can be therapeutic for him in getting off a lot that he has build up in side, he has been expressing it to me and has made me get a better feeling of how he feel about life and family especially my mother because she has been bios between my two boys.

But Jack has gotten this idea that it is okay to smoke weed and I hope no one is feeding it to him in those projects. I know Jack loves his grandmother and great grandmother and has this

idea if he becomes a drug dealer he can make money and get them out of the projects and I know were these ideas are coming from, especially that he is around this type of environment daily living in those projects are being influential in his curiosity of getting money especially since it is hard for them to come by.

Maybe you can explain to Jack a little more in the direction he should go and not follow those people he sees everyday, because he's only going to end up where his mother and me are. I always write him and try to tell him how important education is in his life so he can become a real man and make everyone proud of him, especially me.

I appreciate your time and the encouragement you are providing to my son and I only hope that we can keep him focus because it's difficult and miserable when you are not able to be a total guidance in your kid's life. I will be getting him when I come home and being apart

of his life because I suffered the same growing up not having a father in my life and I don't want Jack to hate me like I've hated my father for the way he treated me.

I'm not able to receive Polaroid pictures, any other type of picture I can receive even printed off the computer or developed. Thank you, and any time you wish to write me, or let me know what's going on in Jack's life, I appreciate it.

(Unsigned)

Jack's father's letter reiterated everything I have been telling my boys for years, and I hoped one day we could meet and maybe work out some type of presentation he could provide for my students. His thoughts seemed clear and his heart and mind were in the right place. The following morning, I pulled Jack outside and confessed to him that I'd written to his father and that I had

received a letter back from him. I explained again about my own experiences with having family in prison. We talked for a long time, and I offered to let Jack read the letter from his father. He was excited, and I joked with him that he could read it if he promised not to rip it up. He extended his hand and said, "Deal!" Jack and I continued to write to his father, and we both were excited when his letters came. We often shared the letters, letting each other read what Jack's father had said to his son and his son's teacher. Jack appreciated the honesty, and I appreciated Jack's trust, as his father's letters to him were often filled with statements of love, hope, and concern.

Jack's negative environment and survival instincts got the best of him toward the end of the school year. During a routine drug test required of his probation he "peed hot," meaning he failed his drug test. While the marijuana in his system was not of a main concern to his probation officer, the cocaine was. When his probation officer told Jack

that he had tested positive for cocaine -- which he had confided to me that he had been using for nearly the whole school year when I confronted him about his mood swings – he ran from the probation office and stayed on the run. He evaded police custody for months, and when he was finally caught, he was placed in foster care in lieu of Juvenile Detention. Since his original detention was in a different county, I did not get a chance to see Jack during his brief incarceration before he was shipped off to foster care.

Chapter Twelve
Breaking and Entering

Matthew rolled over and woke me up. He was pleasant, well rested and wanted to play. I'd only been asleep a couple of hours, and my whole body ached.

"Ya wanna do a puzzle?" he asked in a hoarse whisper.

"Hold on," I squeaked. I knew I had to wake up before he threw a tantrum. If Matthew didn't get his way with me, he would scream and wake up Bobby, and that would be worse than getting out of bed exhausted. Bobby loved and coddled Matthew to the same degree that he hated and tortured me. I have tried to work it out myself, and I even asked Debbie before she died, but there was no real reason. It's just the way it was. I crawled gently from the bed and laid myself out on the floor beside Matthew where he had spread the pieces of the Star Wars puzzle. We had put together this puzzle hundreds of times, and we

were both excited each time we saw the finished picture on the floor. We lay together on the floor, flipping the pieces face up without talking. We rarely spoke to each other inside the apartment. Fitting together the pieces, we were lost in the task as the puzzle came together. The door opened, and the silence was broken. We both snapped to attention. Scrambling to our feet, we heard Debbie's voice before she entered the room.

"Matthew, get dressed if you're gonna play. Greg come here. Bobby wants you." She looked nervous as she stretched her arm toward me. I hesitated but knew there was no escape. I walked to the door and followed her out without reaching for her hand.

"It's gonna be alright. We just need you to cook for us real quick," she whispered.

Bobby was sitting on the couch in the living room. The television was on, but he wasn't watching. His legs were kicked out as if he had

collapsed into position. He looked over his right shoulder at Debbie and me coming toward him. Without a word, he raised his mighty arm over his head and pointed to the stove. Turning into the kitchen area, I saw the milk crates already stacked in position in front of the oven door. I climbed up into my place and hiked up my underwear. I was too little to reach the stove on my own, so I used three milk crates as steps. The bag of heroin sat on the counter next to the works I had been taught to use about a year earlier. At first I had been clumsy and wasted Bobby's dope and therefore his money. He sold heroin out of the apartment and always had a large stash on hand, but easily became angry when I cooked it too long and made it worthless. The beatings that followed each mistake taught me to be more careful and I soon learned how to cook, load, and spike heroin. Cooking it up and loading the needle were routine and automatic.

Spiking the needle into Debbie and Bobby always made me nervous.

I leaned over to my right and turned the faucet on to a soft drizzle. I caught some water with an old glass eyedropper and quickly turned the water off. Leaning back to the stove, I turned on the front burner and picked up the pot, a straightened paperclip wrapped around a large metal bottle cap. I cooked up the heroin and water and loaded it into the syringe. Debbie came to me quickly and grabbed the syringe from my hand. With the job done, I turned off the burner and climbed down from the crates. I stood motionless, waiting for a sign of what to do next. Would I have to spike them too, or could I go back to the puzzle?

Bobby was already tied off when Debbie handed him the needle. She spun her head and her wild red hair flew in front of her eyes. She brushed it aside and looked at me, frantically waving me

away back to the bedroom. No words were ever spoken.

Back in the room, Matthew was dressed and the puzzle was put away. I wondered if he'd let me sleep if I got back into bed.

"We can't go out yet," I told him. "Did you finish the puzzle?"

"Yeah. You gettin' dressed?"

"I wanna go back to bed." I hung my head and feared his response.

"I'm gonna play Men, I don't care what you do." It was then that I noticed the action figures set up on the floor by the closet. I got into bed and curled into a ball. I pressed my knees into my face trying to block out the sunlight flooding the curtain-less windows. Bobby and Debbie would be out for a while, and I knew we weren't allowed to leave the room until they came to get us. The coast was clear. I fell asleep quickly.

"Let's go assholes, we got work!" The door closed as quickly as it had opened.

Bobby's voice woke me from sleep. When I opened my eyes, I saw Matthew asleep on the floor where he'd been playing. My body still ached, but I felt better from the sleep. Crawling from bed, I dragged myself slowly to the closet. I pulled on my pants and found a shirt. Matthew was already out the door, as I pulled the shirt down over my bruised belly. I grabbed my sneakers and walked into the living room. Debbie stood fully dressed in a colorful blouse and jeans. Her platform shoes made her seem large and dangerous. Bobby was sailing through the small apartment, gathering the familiar tools that remained scattered among the mess in the room. On the couch sat two men I had never seen before. They passed a joint between them, and I watched as they flipped the ashes on their pant legs. Bobby ignored them, as he dumped tools onto the couch beside them; they didn't move or seem to recognize that he was there

either. Matthew and I stood silently watching and waiting.

"Don't leave. As soon as we get back, we'll split up what we got and I'll give you the car. It won't be a couple hours. Don't let anyone in." Bobby barked at the two men, but they just sat there inattentively.

"Gotdamn it, what'd I just say?"

"Fuck man, I heard ya. Don't let anyone in. Got it. I need that car tonight, don't lose it." The man never looked at Bobby as he spoke.

Bobby walked in front of the two men and bent down to put his face in theirs.

"Don't leave this fuckin room. I *will* be back." He raised his hand, and I thought he was going to hit them, but he just grabbed the joint and hit it a couple times before passing it back.

Debbie handed him a duffel bag from behind the couch, and he frantically jammed all of the tools into it before zipping it up.

"You got everything?"

"Where are the keys?"

"Gimme the keys." Bobby put his large hand out in front of the men. One of them dropped the keys and looked up for the first time.

"We'll be here, have fun."

Bobby heaved the bag from the couch with his right hand and slung it over his shoulder. As he walked around the couch, he seemed to notice Matthew and me standing there by Debbie. He walked toward us and reached out and stroked Matthew's silky blonde hair.

"You ready for some work? It'll be quick and fun." His eyes sparkled as he spoke to Matthew. Without looking at me, he swung the duffel bag into my chest and demanded, "Carry this shit." With Matthew's small blonde head cradled in his left hand, Bobby guided him past Debbie and toward the front door.

"Woman, get yer ass over here and let's go," his voice was calm but impatient. Matthew looked up at him with awe and admiration. Debbie glided to

the door and reached in front of Bobby and Matthew to undo the multiple locks and chains on the door. When the last chain dangled from its cradle, Bobby took control and opened the door. Still guiding Matthew by his head, he walked out the door. Debbie trailed behind, and I followed, closing the door behind me. I could hear the door being locked and the chains fastened, as I started down the steps. I hefted the duffel bag filled with hammers, pry bars, wrenches and screwdrivers down the three flights of stairs, as Bobby laughed with Matthew and Debbie about the "new" car. Outside, the day was bright, and my eyes hurt from the glare. Just outside the doorway of the building sat a Volkswagen Beetle that Bobby was showing off to Matthew. There was pride in his laughter. As I approached the car, Bobby turned toward me, grabbed the bag from my hands and threw it in the back seat next to Matthew.

"Get in," he ordered. The enthusiasm I had heard earlier was gone when he spoke to me. I

resented Matthew for the difference in our treatment.

Bobby had a hard time getting the car into reverse, and he began to get angry. He yelled at the car, and he yelled at the two men in the apartment for stealing it. The car jerked backward, and I hit my head on the side window. Bobby turned to look at me and laughed. Suddenly he was happy again. I cowered in the seat, holding my head while trying to hide from his view.

We drove in silence for a while, and when I finally looked out the window, I saw trees lining the streets, and houses with lawns. We were nowhere near the Village, and I knew what was coming. Bobby pulled the car over in front of an elegant apartment building with bushes beneath the windows of the lower apartments and a fence around the lush green lawn. I didn't like being so far from home.

"This place has a few condos on each floor. You two run down the hall and knock on each door as you pass by. The stairs are at the end of the hall, hide under there and count what doors get answered. Got it?"

"Okay," Matthew and I replied in unison.

"We'll be in in a minute. Don't say a word inside that building. Take the bag with you. Go!"

Debbie turned in her seat and looked at us from behind large brown sunglasses. I wondered if she could really see us. She reached back and rubbed each of our shaggy heads as we got out of the car. I lugged the bag over my shoulder with both hands.

Matthew and I took off running as soon as we hit the sidewalk. We knew we had to look like two wild kids playing a game to make this work. We raced up the sidewalk, but I lagged behind under the weight of the bag. Matthew jumped up the small concrete steps to the large front door of the building. He slammed his right shoulder into it

while turning the knob, trying to make as much noise as possible. If there were any sleepers in the building, we needed to wake them up. He threw the door open wide and waited for me to make it up the steps. Sore and encumbered, I was moving as quickly as possible, but I could see the frustration on his face.

"Come on," Matthew prodded. He glared at me and then smiled, as he looked behind me to the car.

His impatience didn't help me carry the bag, but I knew Bobby and Debbie were watching, so I tried to quicken my pace. At a slow hobble, I made it up the steps and into the building. There were a few doors on each side of the short, wide hallway. Suddenly energized, we ran down the hall and banged on each door. Matthew got all the doors on the left, and I hit the ones on the right, swinging the heavy bag into each. There was a loud metallic clang each time the bag of tools rammed into the center of a door. Running

as fast as we could, Matthew and I collided at the end of the hall. Slinging the bag under first, we dove under the stairwell and kept quiet just as we'd been told. We poked our heads out trying not to laugh so we could count any doors that opened. Not a single one of them opened and we heard no noise. Leaving the tools beneath the stairs we ran out and hit each door two more times, once going and once coming, then we were back under the stairs. Still nothing.

Debbie walked into the building, "Boys, are you in here? I saw you run in here. Quit playing around!" She was putting on her best concerned parent act just in case someone was coming or looking out a door. Matthew and I appeared from beneath the stairs and reported what happened with a shrug. Several seconds later, Bobby strolled in and eyed the three of us clustered at the end of the hall. Debbie gave him the bag and the all clear.

Matthew ran up the stairs and took his post at the top of the stairs. If anyone came while Bobby was breaking in, he was to run down the stairs as loudly as possible. The three of us walked down the hall to the first apartment door. I took my post at the front door. Bobby chose the door closest to the entrance and knocked on it himself. After a few seconds of silence, he unzipped the duffel bag and pulled out the flat pry bar, then lowered the bag to the ground. Debbie knelt by Bobby's side and handed tools up as needed. As I stared out the front door, I heard the metal door pop open quickly under Bobby's brute force. I turned and saw Debbie pulling pillowcases from the duffel bag, then zipping up the bag and tossing it inside the apartment. She waved to me and gestured for me to get my brother. I ran quickly up the first set of stairs to the landing and waved to Matthew to come down. Bracing myself against the rail, I slid slowly to the bottom of the

stairs. Matthew came bouncing behind me, still trying to wake the residents.

The apartment smelled of powder and dust, there were no food smells like I was used to. The houses and apartments we broke into with Bobby always smelled this way. Debbie handed each of us a pillowcase and we were let loose. Bobby had trained us well, and we kept in good practice in the art of burglary. Matthew and I were in charge of packing the obvious items of value. We stole silverware, candlesticks, jewelry, and any money we found in plain sight. Bobby had taught us the secret places people hide their valuables. He was almost always right. In each room of the large apartment we dumped all the shiny items into our pillowcases. Bobby went directly to the bedrooms. Debbie hit the bathrooms, looking for prescription drugs.

Bobby emerged from a bedroom, stuffing his front pocket. He called to Matthew excitedly,

"Drop that bag son and come to daddy for a minute."

Glowing with pride, Matthew placed his clinking pillowcase on a couch and strutted into the kitchen. I moved extra slowly through the living room, as I spied Bobby's tender attention to Matthew.

"Get up there and find us somethin' good boy," his voice full of encouragement as he carefully thrust Matthew up above his head to search the high cabinets. Matthew swept his hands and eyes across the top of the cabinet.

"Over there," Matthew said, pointing to the other end.

Bobby strode effortlessly to the opposite end of the cabinet with Matthew still held in midair above his head. Matthew pulled down a small box and was lovingly lowered to the ground. Diverting my gaze, I began throwing everything in sight into my pillowcase. Debbie continued her search in the bedrooms for jewelry and anything

else of value. Bobby stood motionless in the kitchen, rifling through the small box and hastily stuffed its contents into his pockets. There was no television or stereo, and that made Bobby mad. He began to curse whoever lived there and stomped around the living room stabbing a screwdriver through the glass of all of the picture frames. It was time to move on.

We moved directly across the hall, trying to stay close to the front door of the building. Bobby pounded a crowbar against the bottom of the door, and I could hear the echo inside the apartment. He popped the door with ease, and we were inside again. Debbie moved quickly to the back bedroom, and I heard a scream. Looking up from my pillowcase, I saw Debbie slowly backing into the room. In front of her was a white haired old woman in a nightgown. She was wearing a heavy pearl necklace and a funny looking hat. She didn't seem scared or even alarmed that we were there. She was mumbling

something that I could not make out. Before I knew what was happening, I saw Bobby swing the crowbar across the woman's face. Blood sprayed from the gash instantly. She collapsed to the floor before the crowbar was at Bobby's side.

"Beat the hell out'er, Matt, get'er!" Bobby commanded.

Matthew attacked her with a ferocity I knew well. He had learned from Bobby. Matthew liked it. He hit her over and over again until her eyes closed. Bobby had stood and watched as his favorite son beat the old woman unconscious before moving around the room looking for more loot. I, too, stood watching, unable to move until Bobby noticed and ordered me back to work. In a moment of greed and disgust I snatched the pearls from the old woman's throat and stuffed them in my pillowcase. Matthew never stopped hitting her.

Hoisting the television from its place, Bobby made a quick exit to the car outside. The three of

us followed with Debbie carrying the extra bags. We left the old woman's apartment with her lying in a bloody pool on the floor, not knowing or caring if she was alive or dead. We loaded ourselves, and Bobby's loot, into the car and fled back to the Village. Bobby raced back onto the interstate, as the car filled with cigarette smoke and laughter. The radio came on for the first time, and Debbie sang along while she grabbed Bobby's thigh. He looked at her and yelled, "Bitch, I love you!"

The radio blared, as we returned to the safety of the Village. After racing through the maze of buildings, the car came to a screeching halt, inches from the brick façade of our building. Bobby was still laughing, as he jumped from the car. He threw the seat forward for Matthew to climb out and then reached in to grab the television. Matthew and I grabbed our pillowcases, while Debbie grabbed the rest. Into the dark and musty building we ran. Matthew

and I lugged our pillowcases one step at a time,
making more noise than we should have, but the
makeshift bags were much too heavy for us to
carry up three flights of stairs with any grace. I
heard Bobby kicking the door and yelling for the
men inside to open the door. There was more
noise from above, and then one of the men
descended the stairs and grabbed the pillowcases
from Matthew and me and threw one over each
shoulder with a smile.

"Yer a hell uva kid," he said to Matthew before
running back up the stairs.

"Race ya," was all Matthew said as he darted up
the remaining stairs to the apartment. The door
was locked when we got there. Matthew did the
special knock, and the door was opened.

There was a party going on in the tiny apartment,
and Matthew and I were suddenly in the middle
of it. The two men we had left in the apartment
were digging through the loot, as Bobby plugged
in the television. The new one was much larger

and nicer than ours, and everyone was easily excited by it.

The men were each making piles out of the pillowcases and commenting on which fence in the Village would take which pieces and how much could be gained from taking it out of the city. With the television in place, Bobby grabbed a pillowcase and dumped it in front of him. Debbie passed out beers to each of the men.

"Matt, get yer ass over here," he called.

Matthew bounced over to Bobby's side, smiling. "Yeah?"

"This yer bag boy?"

"I think so."

Pulling from the bottle of beer he'd just been handed, Bobby took a breath and yelled proudly, "Gotdamn that's a helluva job boy," as he cuddled Matthew close to his side.

"Baby, get this man a beer. He done earned it today. This the best you ever done. I'm proud of my little man today," Bobby beamed as he turned

to his friends. "You shoulda seen tha way he beat dat bitch in dat house today. I'll tell ya, this sonuvabitch has learned from the best!" He said to no one in particular.

Debbie looked at Bobby without saying a word. He did not notice and never turned his gaze from his young protégé. She moved away and wandered stoically to the refrigerator and pulled out another beer. She moved painfully back to the living room and handed her oldest son a beer. I sat behind the couch and watched the scene unfold.

Sitting in his high back chair, Bobby launched his mission to turn the loot into cash and drugs. The phone rang each time it was set back in its cradle. Purveying his bounty as he spoke, I heard Bobby describe his take to the various callers. The deals were sealed, and Bobby was pleased. He shuffled the loot quickly and divided it into distinct piles. Matthew and I were ordered to take it carefully, pile by pile, into the spare bedroom. When all the

piles were moved and the living room floor was clear again, we waited for our next order. Matthew picked up his beer and retreated to Bobby's side. Debbie sat on the couch, rolling joints. The two men sat on either side of Debbie, talking frantically. The room had become a frenzy of excitement.

Rhythmic knocks brought men and women flooding into the apartment. Before Matthew finished his beer, the room was filled with people, smoke and music. Some of the people I had seen before, but they did not acknowledge that I was in the room. Matthew was sitting on Bobby's lap, as he recounted his beating of the old woman. "Daddy knocked her down and I jumped on top of her and beat on her till she din't move," he bragged, "she was bleedin' all over the floor, and it was gettin' on me so I got up and kicked her," he paused and took a sip of his beer. Bobby nodded his head like a proud papa and rubbed Matthew's shaggy blonde hair. Bobby grabbed

the empty beer bottle from his hand and held it above his head, "That's my boy. I love this little mufucka!" he exclaimed.

He turned his gaze in my direction and yelled, "Hey, quit being a worthless piece of shit an' get yer brother a beer."

I leapt from my haven behind the couch and scurried to the fridge. I grabbed a bottle and hurried back to Bobby. As I handed him the bottle, he scolded me quietly: "That aint fo' me asshole, give it da him." Matthew smirked, as I handed him the beer. The party gathered around Bobby's chair, begging to hear Matthew recount his story over and over. It changed with each telling, getting more graphic each time, until finally he bragged about having kicked the old woman to death. No one seemed to notice the inconsistencies, as they drank and smoked. Some snorted cocaine from a platter on the table in the middle of the room. The party only laughed as Matthew got drunk and rested his head on

Bobby's giant shoulder. Debbie whispered in Bobby's ear, and he shook Matthew awake.

"Get up, you all right."

Matthew's head rolled around, and he hopped down onto the floor. Matthew landing firmly on his feet elicited applause from the room. Bobby got up and moved into the small hall area.

"Tony wants some; I said not tonight, but I think you need to tell him," she pleaded.

"If Tony wants some give him some, ya know he got tha money. Where he at?" Bobby's eyes shot across the room.

Tony was a frequent visitor, and I knew him well. He was a tall, slender brother with a large afro. Always dressed in a flashy half-open shirt and tight pants, he wore the same brown boots as Bobby. Now he stood in the center of the room, holding the platter of cocaine to his face, with his eyes trained on Debbie.

Bobby stepped toward me and grabbed my arm, dragging me to my mother. "Take him with you, he just in the way out here."

I watched, as Bobby moved toward Tony and patted him on the back. Debbie pulled my head around to face her.

"I love you. You know that, right?" It wasn't a question. Her familiar slurred speech and glassy eyes told me that she was high. "Go sit in the room like your daddy said. You don't have to watch if you don't want." She pushed me down the short hall toward her bedroom.

I grabbed a bed sheet from the floor and curled up in the chair. I pulled it over my head and covered my body. Without warning, I heard Debbie and Tony enter the room.

Huddled under the sheet, I pressed my hands over my ears, but I could still hear my mother having sex. The room began to fill with the rank odor of sweat. The noises got louder, and I couldn't keep out the sound.

"Shit baby, I jus' cain't cum. You gon' have ta owe me one when I aint done so much blow sweetheart. Ya man undastand," Tony declared. "Yeah, baby. Sure," she agreed without protest. The door opened and closed again. Debbie pulled the sheet from my head, "Let's go out to the party baby. It'll be fun." She was sweaty, naked and out of breath as she yanked me from the chair.

I pulled away from her and let the sheet release into her hands. She wrapped herself in it and wiped the sweat away before grabbing her dress from the floor. I rolled myself from the chair after Debbie strapped into her shoes. She held her hand out to me from across the bed, and I made my way to her. Debbie looked down at me with her mouth silently agape.

With my hand in hers, she opened the door slowly and crept out smoothly, silently closing the door behind me. In a single motion she opened the door to my bedroom and flung me into the

darkness. The door clicked closed, and I scrambled to my bed. Fully dressed and exhausted, I made my way through the darkness and climbed into bed. Sleep fell upon me instantly.

Chapter Thirteen
Mirror Image

Brandon transferred in from another state, but his records were not readily available. At least I had warning that he was coming. He had been enrolled several days before I ever saw his face. Calls home only gave vague insight into his absences, but his parent assured me he would be in any day. When he walked in on his first day, my shock could not have been any more apparent.

His parents walked him to class, escorted by the principal. She made her introductions and made a hasty departure. Before me stood the boy's father, a lanky man, weathered and hardened by time. He bore the tattooed arms of an ex-con. His wife wavered beside him, speaking too quickly for her seemingly intoxicated state. I guessed methamphetamines based on the smell, thinly disguised by the pungent odor of cigarette smoke.

They were fresh transplants from the north, having moved here with the promise of a manufacturing job in a local automotive plant. He was sick. They'd all been sick. They had trouble finding their way around town. Their excuses for their son's absences were different now than they had been on the phone. My previous suspicions were immediately heightened. The boy hid behind his mother's legs, clinging to them as if for support. She reached around and pulled him forward. And there he was; my latest student could have been my brother, an identical twin 20 years my junior. His appearance uncovered innumerable repressed memories of my own neglect and abuse and I recognized the signs as he stood in front of me. Something was wrong with this scenario and I was determined to find out what.

He was shabbily dressed and barely conscious, with dark black rings around his eyes. His shaggy brown curly hair lay in tangles around his pudgy

face, atop a frail and gaunt frame. He didn't acknowledge my presence when I introduced myself. He just stared blankly. Normally I would have reacted more forcefully to such a response, but given the scene, and my suspicions, I let it all slide. His parents told me that there had been some issues getting his transfer records due to some money that was owed to his previous school, but the records should be coming shortly as soon as the check they had mailed was cashed. I made a mental note to call the boy's school as soon as possible. They said their goodbyes, to which the boy did not respond, as he had not responded to me.

The boy entered class and sat in the seat I had prepared for him. Without asking him to stand, I introduced him to the class. The boys turned and looked at him in wonder. There were several comments as to his consciousness but nothing rude or disrespectful. The boys had gained a modicum of respect and empathy, and I was

proud of their composure and restraint. Brandon stared blankly at nothing in particular, as I informed him of the rules of the class and began our daily routine.

Within moments of our math lesson, the first of the day, Brandon was asleep sitting straight up in his chair, his head hanging loosely backward, his mouth wide open. I walked toward him and lifted his head forward, but he did not wake. I shook him gently, but still he displayed no signs of life. I checked his pulse at his neck. It was faint but present. I sent for Michelle and Renee. Renee came in shortly after the messenger, and I filled her in on the "Brandon Situation."

I lifted him out of his seat and laid him gently down on a set of beanbag chairs placed end to end on the floor away from any possible traffic. Renee got on the phone and made several calls to Brandon's former school in attempts to gain some insight into the boy's history. The class worked diligently on their math assignment, while I

searched the Internet for any public records of his parents. To my distress, I learned that his father was on probation, in addition to having several active warrants back in his home state. The latest warrant issued only days before Brandon was registered in our school. Renee's digging uncovered similarly unsettling news, but she got the school to fax the records we wanted. The story I had been told earlier turned out to be untrue. Brandon had never been withdrawn from school and they were thankful for the call and happy to oblige. The principal offered as much information as was available, which was more than we expected or wanted to know. When she returned to my classroom, Renee brought Michelle in with her, and we compared notes and took the rest of the day to devise a plan. Meanwhile, Brandon slept through his entire first day of school, resting peacefully on the beanbags. As spokesman for the group and teacher of the class, I went to the principal and explained the

"Brandon Situation" in all its gory detail. We needed a medical release signed, which was standard procedure, but this was not a standard situation. While it wasn't too far off, it was an uneasy predicament, as Michelle and Renee typically would drive the medical release around during the school day, getting it signed by the parents and then to the doctor. We were all concerned with sending the ladies to the home of a wanted felon. I was eager to get the situation taken care of, so I volunteered to head over after school, but I wanted to inform my principal before taking action. She offered to accompany me, but I declined.

The yard was a minefield of discarded toys and trash. Walking to the door of the small house, I caught sight of a smatter of dirty diapers by the front steps. I had called ahead, so when I knocked on the door it was opened quickly, and the thin man from earlier that day greeted me with a smile. He opened the door, and I saw several

older teenagers, too old to be the children of Brandon's parents, scurry through the room. The rancid odor of recently burned crack cocaine wafted from the house as Brandon's father stepped outside. Clumsily smoking a menthol cigarette, the man stumbled down the steps, trying to talk me away from the house, insisting that he had relatives over unexpectedly and needed to get back inside. There were two vehicles in the driveway, and one of them was mine. I spoke with him as he led me down the thin footpath back to my Jeep. When we got there, I unbuttoned and pulled off my long sleeve shirt, exposing my t-shirt and tattooed arms. Throwing the shirt into the truck, I asked for a cigarette. His eyes went immediately to my tattoos, as I had hoped they would. His mood lightened as he stuffed two cigarettes in his mouth, lit them both, and handed one to me. We made our way slowly back toward the house.

Attentively I listened to his troubles and complaints about the "white trash ghetto" he had been living in before moving into the predominantly Black neighborhood we were standing in. He said he preferred it here in the south and would be staying here for a while. I asked if Brandon had said anything about his day at school. Now chain-smoking, the man told a fascinating tale about how Brandon had come home talking about all of the fun he had at school. Eager to get inside the house, I mentioned the form that needed to be signed. After bumming another cigarette, I asked if we could go inside. He lit another for me, and we laughed about nothing as we smoked.

The small house reeked of crack cocaine. Two bedroom doors that would lead into the room were closed. Two half-clothed children ran around the living room—a cluttered mess of filthy clothes, broken toys, and animal feces. A baby was perched in a highchair in a small adjoining

kitchen. Brandon sat awake but motionless on the couch. He was more alert than I'd seen earlier in the day.

"Hey Mr. Love," he said from the couch. I was surprised he knew my name.

"Hi Brandon. How are you?" I asked.

"You wanna see my kittens?" He asked cheerfully.

"Not now Bran, your teacher's gotta get going. We just have to sign some papers." His dad answered. Turning to me, he asked for the paper. I handed him the form and a pen. He signed it on top of the television without a word. "There you go," he said as he handed the paper and pen back to me. He stepped toward the door. I had seen enough. I reached for the door, but he was more eager, and he opened it before I could grab the knob.

"Goodbye Brandon. I'll see you in the morning." I said to the boy who looked so much like me that

I was anxious to get away. Unwelcome memories washed over me.

He waved from the couch as I walked out the door. I turned and shook his father's hand and thanked him for the cigarettes. He offered one for the ride and I accepted, hoping it might calm my nerves.

The next morning, Brandon arrived on the bus with the other students. Being the shortest of the students, he stood at the front of my line as instructed. He led the line toward the class with a meandering shuffle. Silently he went to his seat and sat down. Seeing him awake relieved the anxiety that had haunted me overnight. Greeting and talking with the boys took my mind away from Brandon's home and family. As we started in with our work, Brandon conked out as he had the day before: sitting upright, head back, mouth open. The other boys looked, but did not say a word. I prodded him awake. He closed his mouth and brought his head down to look at me.

"Do you want to lie down?" I asked kindly.

"Mmhm," he muttered.

"Can you get up for me and walk over there?" I asked, pointing to the beanbag chairs still in position. He tumbled from the chair and made it to the makeshift bed just before his legs gave out. He was asleep before his head hit the cushion. I found a beach towel among the random items in my closet and draped it over him. Taking off his shoes to make him more comfortable, I noticed his socks were filthy, as if he had played in the mud before putting on his shoes. I rolled his socks from his feet and placed them on a piece of paper. I sent one of my boys to the classroom across the hall that had a washer and dryer with instructions to have them cleaned. The other boys watched in bewilderment as I pampered the young boy with a tenderness they had not witnessed from me before. I ignored their confused stares as if nothing had happened.

Standing back at the front of the class, I went back to our lesson. My heart wasn't in it.

The signed medical release on my desk was eating at my conscience. Impatiently waiting for Michelle and Renee, I tried to busy myself with the intricacies of basic math. Finally the ladies arrived, and I told the story of my visit. At my insistent urging, they took off for the doctors, and the waiting began. The morning crawled into the afternoon without a word from the ladies. Brandon regained consciousness after lunch, but he was slow in achieving any level of energy required for regular schoolwork. His socks had come back clean and dry, and I had replaced them while he slept. When he woke with his shoes off, he put them on without a word. The class lined up to head outside for our daily hour of physical training. He sat on the sidelines, as my other students and I did our workout. After working up a sweat with calisthenics and yoga in the warm sun, the boys began their run. I went

over to Brandon and asked him to walk with me. Surprisingly he got up eagerly, and we trotted behind the line. He started talking immediately. He told me of his friends up North, the drive to Tennessee and the people he lives with. His mind seemed to be working at hyper speed, and he could not keep on a single topic for more than a few moments. I tried to ask questions, but he didn't seem to hear them, as he was talking so fast. I decided to walk and listen. He didn't need any encouragement to open up.

Toward the end of the day, the ladies came back but did not have the medical information I was hoping for. They had gotten caught up with another assignment for another client and were lucky to have gotten the medical release where it needed to go. Though disappointed, I understood their predicament, and I thanked them for running around for me. Luckily, I had my conversation with Brandon to reflect on. His rambling flood of information was a lot to digest

and dissect. While his parents had proved to be untrustworthy, Brandon's stories seemed to be linear and sensible. His steady stream of speech made me believe at least the majority of his story. A few days went by, and Brandon came to school in his typical zombified-state. We developed a routine in which he would sleep in the morning and get his academics in the afternoon while the other students were involved in independent activities. Each day I would take off his shoes and have his socks washed while he slept. One day he came in particularly dirty. The ladies went to the school's clothes closet where lost and found items, in addition to donated items, wound up. They found some clothes that fit Brandon and had him change his clothes in the restroom before he went down for his morning nap. We sent his clothes across the hall to be cleaned. The day got ahead of us all, and before we knew it, it was time for the kids to go home. Someone realized that Brandon did not have his clothes, so we ran next

door, grabbed his clothes, and stuffed them in his backpack as we shuffled him along to the bus.

First thing in the morning, I was called to the office, and as I approached I saw Brandon and his father through the large glass walls of the office. Brandon's father was holding the clothes we had sent him home in the day before. As soon as I stepped into the office the yelling intensified. My principal promptly stopped the man's public tirade and suggested we step into her office where the three of us could speak privately. Her presence was very commanding, and she was exceptionally effective at controlling the most out-of-control parents.

In her office, Brandon's father attempted to yell, but was deftly quieted by the principal. In softer tones, he expressed his frustration over his child coming home in clothes that were not his, while his own clothes were stuffed into his bag. When he stopped, my principal spoke of the high standards her teachers have for their students and

the positive impact a clean appearance can have on a child. She spoke clearly and calmly, showing a lot of respect for the man and his feelings. Then she turned to me, as if to suggest it was my turn. I took responsibility for having sent Brandon home in strange clothes but assured his father that they were new and clean. I also told him that we had cleaned Brandon's clothes at school because he had gotten dirty and we did not want him to have to go through his day wearing dirty clothes. Insinuating that he had gotten dirty at school, not that he had come to school in such a condition. With my vague explanation, I was sure not to blame, offend, or upset anyone. And it worked. Brandon's father thanked us for our time, apologized for the misunderstanding and exited the office. As we all walked out, the principal and I noticed that the man had walked by his son without speaking to or even looking at him. I woke Brandon up and walked him to class after thanking my principal for her assistance.

Then the day came in which our medical release form had worked its magic. Faxes began to roll in concerning the doctors the family had visited with Brandon and the medications he was prescribed. His prescriptions were not the same medications that the parents had told us he was taking, more accurately, he was being prescribed and dispensed more medications than the family admitted to giving him and more than Brandon had told us that he took each morning. As expected, the prescriptions were for evening medications that were being given in the morning to make him drowsy. Brandon had told me repeatedly that he stayed up most of the night while his parents entertained people from the neighborhood. He had told stories of people coming and going at all hours throughout the night, and because he slept on the couch, he was not able to get much sleep. His parents, he said, gave him his medicine in the morning so he would sleep through school, so as not to discuss

what happened in the house at night. He too had been coached.

When he first told the ladies and me, this fact it seemed like a plausible story, but now with the verification that he was indeed being prescribed evening medications, his story became significantly more credible. With the situation teetering on a viable case of abuse and neglect, our team went back to the principal and informed her of the new developments. Together we decided to conduct another home visit, but this time we would go as a group and present ourselves as if we were making a typical home visit. There would be no phone call beforehand. A few days went by, and we solidified our plan. We got our story straight for the family regarding why the principal had accompanied the classroom staff to the home. When the day came, the anxiety I felt after the first visit returned. The day went by too quickly, and I wanted to keep Brandon after school, so he would not be at home

while we descended on his family. I put him on the bus with the rest of the students, and accompanied by our principal, the ladies and I drove out toward Brandon's house.

We met up at a restaurant close to the house and piled into the principal's SUV. We drove over in palpable anticipation. As we pulled into the driveway, we noticed several cars in the driveway with various out of state plates. The yard was in even more disarray than before. More toys, more trash. We paraded up the walk and onto the porch. I knocked on the door. There was a quiet commotion inside the house. A young girl in tattered clothes opened the door. By the look on her face she recognized me, but I told her who I was anyway. She turned around and shouted, "It's Mr. Love, Brandon's teacher." I heard a door open and Brandon's father's face appeared around the door.

"Hey, uh, what's up?" He said shakily.

My principal stepped forward, and stood in front of me, introducing herself. The door came open against its will.

"Can we come in?" She asked as she pushed by him leading us all into the house. The room was crowded with five adults standing just inside the door. We positioned ourselves around the room. I walked closest to the couch where Brandon was sitting in the same spot I saw him in last time. He had an electronic football game in his hands. He looked up and put the game down.

"Hey Mr. Love. Do you wanna play Monopoly?" He asked as he leapt from the couch. "Not now Bran. We don't have time for that." His father's voice had an edge of uneasiness. He backed toward the bedroom door closest to him. The girl that had opened the door was now in the kitchen making dinner. Brandon ignored his father and maneuvered between the adults to a crumbling stack of games and boxes by the television. He

found the game and brought it back to the couch where he proceeded to set it up.

"What piece do you wanna be, Mr. Love?" Brandon asked as he set out the colorful money.

"I said 'not now' Brandon, put the game away." His father's voice was stern this time. Sadly, Brandon began to pack up the game.

"Brandon, we have that game in class. Tomorrow morning we'll play with the class." I said trying to cheer him.

"I just wanna play with you and me." Brandon replied.

"All right, you got it. You and I will play in the morning. How's that?" I said.

At the promise he smiled my smile. "OK," he said while he packed up the game with enthusiasm.

We spoke with Brandon's father for close to ten minutes, explaining Brandon's sleep and academic issues. We told him that we were concerned and asked if there was anyway we

could help. He declined every service we offered. The young girl in the kitchen called the kids in for dinner. I watched Brandon abandon the game and run to the kitchen. He jumped up into a chair and waited. The girl had cooked dinner for the other kids. She pulled a cookie sheet full of fish sticks out of the oven and placed it on the table. Next to it she slammed down a bottle of ketchup. One of the other children poured a pile of ketchup onto the cookie sheet. The cook dumped a jar of baby food onto the tray of the high chair then lifted the baby from the floor, and placed her into position. The baby fed herself with her hands from the thin pile of mashed food on the tray while the other kids ate fish sticks and ketchup from the cookie sheet. In seconds, they were all done eating. I tried to return my attention to the conversation going on in front of me when I saw several small gray kittens emerge from the kitchen and into the living room.

Brandon's father noticed me looking at the kittens and changed the subject quickly, "Mr. Love, ya want some of them kittens? Take as many as you want. I don't even know how many there are."

"No thanks. I've got a cat of my own. But I appreciate the offer." I said with a smile of satisfaction.

Sensing it was time to go, my principal announced our departure. "Well, we're here if you need us. Just give us a call or stop by the school if you need anything. Anything at all." She smiled her generous smile and extended her hand, which was shaken with enthusiasm.

"Thanks for stopping by. Come by any time. Take care." He said looking around the room as he continued shaking the principal's hand.

We made our exit and piled into the SUV. When the doors were closed, we all spoke at once. Each one of us noticed multiple "red flags" that made us question the safety of not only Brandon, but his siblings as well.

Brandon did not come to school the next day or the next. We all became concerned when the phone number only gave a recording that the number was out of service. Michelle and Renee took a drive across town to check the house. They called from the road to tell me that there were no cars in the driveway, and there were a lot of bags of trash, more than usual, in the front yard that looked like they'd been picked through by wild animals. I asked them to come on back to school so we could think through our next step. When they arrived we decided to call the police and ask them to do a courtesy "welfare check." The officer that performed the check came to the school to tell us that there was no one living at the residence, that and the house appeared to be abandoned. Brandon and his family were gone. We never saw or heard from them again.

Chapter Fourteen
Drinking

The party was over, and I was set to work to clean up the mess. The apartment was covered in the filth and grime of the night before. I had slept through most of the party, which had only just ended when I was woken up and told to start cleaning. The sun shone brightly through the windows, it's heat already fermenting the stench of cigarettes in stale beer, alcohol on the floor, and the elusive smell of vomit and urine that I would later discover soaking into the couch. Debbie tiptoed around the apartment while directing me to do the same. She whispered to me to get all the trash up as quickly and quietly as possible. I moved deftly back and forth from the kitchen to the living room, padding around, picking up trash and emptying ashtrays.

The trashcan in the kitchen was quickly full, and I was not strong enough to lift the bag out. Debbie came over from her chair where she'd been

watching me clean and lifted the bag as I held the can down to muffle the noise. The glass in the bag rattled as Debbie wiggled the bag to the top of the can. She set it down quickly on the floor with a look of terror. While I was sure Bobby was unconscious in his room, both of us knew that he could wake up at any time, and this realization filled us with fear. Debbie lifted the bag and motioned for me to grab the bottom. Together we struggled to get the trash to the door. Debbie was tired and weak and had probably not been to sleep before waking me up, but Debbie was always tired and weak.

We got the bag out the door and down the stairs, leaving it for later. We climbed the steps and found ourselves locked out. I had double-checked the door to make sure it was not locked before we took the trash out. I looked at Debbie and saw that she was crying. I knew that we had woken Bobby, and he had locked us out. Debbie tapped on the door and the sound reverberated through

the stairwell. She took my hand and squeezed it tightly as we stood there waiting for the door to open. The door did not open, and we just stood there. Waiting.

After some time, Debbie tapped again on the door to no avail. Debbie told me to wait by the door while she went back down stairs. I begged for her to take me with her, but she refused and pushed on my shoulders until I was slumped against the door. With a quiet command to stay still, Debbie descended the stairs to go use a neighbor's phone. Shortly after she disappeared, I could hear the phone ringing in the apartment. Finally Bobby picked it up and began to yell into the receiver. The door suddenly flew open, and I collapsed onto the apartment floor. I looked up to see Bobby's half naked form staring down at me with the phone still to his ear. He reached down and dragged me into the apartment.

"Bitch I told you neva leave that fuckin' door open and what tha fuck do you do? What tha

fuck do you do?" He was yelling into the phone, but he was staring down at me. His face was inches from mine, and I could hear Debbie crying on the other end of the phone.

"You betta get yo ass up here before I kill this boy for waking my ass up." He wrapped the curling phone cord around my neck and beat the receiver against my head.

"You little mufucka what tha fuck you doin leavin' that fuckin door open and wakin' me up? What tha fuck you doin?" He punctuated his words with smacks across my face with the telephone receiver. He didn't want an answer; I knew I wasn't supposed to speak. He wanted retaliation for the perceived disrespect and disloyalty.

"Get in that corner and don' you fuckin' move till I tell you!" He pointed to the far corner of the living room, closest to the kitchen. Moments later, Debbie knocked on the door, and Bobby pulled her inside.

He tossed her onto the floor by her hair. She covered her face with her arms and began to cry. I turned around to see what was happening. Bobby saw my movement and stepped quickly toward me, pushing my head into the corner. "Keep your face in this corner and don' you fuckin' move! That's yer problem, you don't fuckin' listen!" He pulled his hand away and slapped the back of my head, bouncing my face against the wall.

Bobby proceeded to beat Debbie while she crawled around on the ground, searching for somewhere to hide. From the corner of my eye, I could see her moving across the floor close to me. Kicking, screaming, punching, screaming, Bobby's attack was unwieldy.

Bobby bent over and spoke into Debbie's ear, "I'm goin' back to bed, and I don't wanna hear another fuckin' sound. DO. YOU. HEAR. ME?"

"Yes." She whispered through her cries, "Not a sound."

"An' dis little bastard does not MOVE *from that corner* until I say so. Do you hear me? Doesn't fuckin' move!" His words were an explosion of brutality.

Her response was inaudible but acceptable, as I heard him tramp back to his room and slam the door. Debbie crept to my side and whispered an apology, telling me I was a good boy for listening. "Just do what you're told. Your dad'll be up soon, and you can go lay down then. It won't be long. I promise." Her promise was as empty as her bloodshot eyes staring at me.

I stood in the corner for hours, trying to keep still until I heard Bobby's bedroom door open. I raised my body and stood as straight as I could manage, leaning my shoulders against the walls that formed the corner. My nose firmly planted in the corner.

"Did he move?" He asked Debbie, referring to me.

"No baby, he's been there the whole time." She said anxiously.

"I wasn't asking you, was I? I was asking him." I heard Matthew climbing on the couch.

"No, he's been there the whole time I think. I haven't been up long but he's been there since I've been watching TV." Matthew reported all he knew to Bobby. He hadn't been awake when the beating happened and didn't know why I was standing in the corner. Surely he didn't care. Since he had been back from the foster home, my life was worse than before he had left. Bobby's rage had built up in the time Matthew was away, and since his return he had been more vicious than ever.

I felt a harsh tug on my head. My neck jerked upward as my head was pulled back. Bobby's breath stunk of vomit and alcohol as he spoke, "I'm goin' out. When I get back ya better be right here in dis fuckin' corner." He slammed my head

back into the corner. I felt blood drip into my eyes.

He announced his departure to Debbie and Matthew. There was a noise from the kitchen where Debbie was sitting. Matthew said his goodbye from the couch. Bobby repeated to Debbie what he had just told me. "He is not to move and you don't leave dis house." He warned as he made his way to the door.

"We need groceries," Debbie said meekly.

"I don' give a shit what you need," he screamed back. "You'll get 'em when I get back so quit yer bitchin'." He lowered his voice and spoke slowly, "If anyone comes you give them what they want, and leave the money in the drawer." With a slam of the door, he was gone. Dropping my shoulders, I slumped against the wall and took a breath. Time went by slowly, and I got weaker standing against the wall. My legs were tired and aching. I switched from leg to leg as each fell asleep from

standing all morning and into the afternoon.

Taking a chance, I called out to Debbie.

"Mom, mom." I whispered into the corner. She

was sitting a few feet away at the kitchen table.

"What do you need baby," she whispered back.

Matthew was still lying on the couch watching

Bewitched, and I could hear his intermittent

laughter. I hoped he would not hear me

whispering to Debbie. Matthew would tell Bobby

that I was talking, and that would be as bad as my

having moved from the corner.

"Mom, I've got to use it." I was dancing in place,

trying not pee my pants. Moving about trying to

keep my legs from falling out from under me had

jostled my bladder, and the urge to go to the

bathroom was unbearable. I whispered again

thinking she hadn't heard me over the TV,

"Mom, I've got to go bad."

"Baby not now. You're father could come home

any minute. You can go when he comes home."

Her reply was slow and quiet, speaking when the TV volume could mask her words.

"Mom, I'm gonna pee my pants if I don't go. I'll go fast. I promise. I've got to go." I was whining, but there was no denying the urgency. If I peed on myself I would be in trouble. If I got caught talking by Matthew and he told Bobby I would be in trouble, if I moved out of the corner I would be in trouble.

Debbie sensed the seriousness of my words. I never whined, or cried, or complained. If I said I needed to go she knew I understood the risk.

"Go. Quick. Then get right back in the corner." She whispered her instruction as she got out of her seat. She walked to the couch, and I passed behind her, hiding my shuffling to the bathroom. She sat down on the end of the couch next to Matthew's head as I made my way up the short hall. I sat down to relieve myself so my legs could rest. As my legs dangled from the seat I heard the door open and I shot upright from the toilet,

urine streaming onto the floor. I pulled up my pants and ran to the corner. I caught Bobby's eye as he was closing the door.

"What. The. Fuck. Are you doing outta dat corner boy." His voice was calm and menacing. I froze in place, still urinating on myself. When he spoke again, he had a perilous smile on his face. "Shit, boy, you're pissing all over yourself." Then the smile disappeared. Debbie stood up. Matthew sat up slightly and twisted his body around to see my urine-soaked pants.

"He had to go to the bathroom, baby. He just now moved. He's been in the corner all day until just now. I promise." She was up and holding one of his forearms. He held a package tucked under one arm and a cigarette in his hand.

"I don' give a shit what he had to do. I told him *and you* that he was not to leave 'at corner," he waved his cigarette at the corner. "What I say aint gotta be listened to? We'll fuckin see abou' dat." He threatened.

He stopped me on my way back to the corner, covering my forehead with the hand that held his cigarette. I could smell the burning end singeing my curly hair. He tilted my head back to face him, "Ya aint gotta go anymore do ya? Yo pants is soakin' ass wet like a baby." He let go of my head and tossed me easily into the corner. His attention turned to Debbie. "Didn't you teach dis boy how to use da toilet? We aint got no money to buy diapers for him too."

Turning his attention back to me, he ordered me to turn around and face him. Cold, afraid, and tired I faced him as instructed.

"Get yer ass in dat bathroom. I'm gonna have ta teach you how ta use da toilet. Lucky for you I gotta piss right now." He motioned me toward the bathroom. My wet pants stuck to my legs, and I had trouble moving. Bobby shoved me down the hall and guided me forcefully into the bathroom where I fell to the ground, slipping in my own urine. Closing and locking the door

behind him, he began to undo his pants. Almost immediately Debbie began pounding on the door. She was crying and begging for Bobby to open the locked door. His determination to teach me a lesson was unfazed by her entreaty.

He undid his pants fully and began to urinate as I watched. "Look at me boy. You see dis?" I looked up at his face from the floor. "Dis how a man use da toilet, not all over hisself or the floor like a baby." He said, noticing the floor smeared wet with my urine. He freed his hand and reached to the sink and grabbed the cup of toothbrushes. Dumping the toothbrushes into the sink he held the cup between himself and the toilet filling the cup. As the last of his urine dripped into the toilet he handed the cup to me. His warm urine splashed onto my face as I tried to hold the wet cup.

"You eva' piss on my floor again I'ma' kick yo ass. If you eva' disobey me when I tell you ta do somethin' I'ma kill you. You undastan'?"

Shaking the warm, wet cup I answered nervously, "Yes."

"Good. Now drink dat shit boy. Drink it. Drink it all." He commanded as he tilted the cup to my mouth. I choked and coughed as the smell hit my nose.

"I said drink dat shit boy. If ya don't drink it I'm gonna give ya somethin' else and you aint gonna like dat either." He looked down at his still open pants and I knew what he meant. He had locked me in the bathroom with him regularly. "Now drink!" His words were unwavering.

I put the cup to my mouth, and Bobby put his hand on the bottom to force the urine down my throat faster. Knowing what was expected I gulped down the contents of the cup. The warm pungent liquid stung my throat as it went down. Bobby laughed and fastened his pants. Holding the dripping cup in front of me I shook once and threw up all over Bobby's legs and feet. Before he could move out of the way in the cramped

bathroom, I threw up again, this time completely soaking his pants so they resembled my own. I felt a fleeting moment of satisfaction. Bobby's stiff hand knocked the cup out of my hand and my body into the wall.

"What da fuck?" He said with his hands in the air. He looked down at himself and pinched his soaking pants pulling them away from his legs. He pulled the door handle, but it didn't budge. He unlocked the door and yanked it open again. He grabbed me by the hair and tossed me into the hallway. He began kicking me down the hall toward my bedroom. He kicked me until my head cracked on the doorjamb to the bedroom. He reached down and threw me into the bedroom.

"You lil' piece a' shit!"

My head rang, but his words were clear. Sprawled on the floor, I was an open target, and he began to hammer the back of my thighs with his vomit-soaked boot. He kicked me into a fetal

ball of submission. My hands covered my face, so I didn't realize he was coming after me until I was off the ground. His strong, callused hands squeezed my limp body as he heaved me over his head. I soared briefly through the air across the room. Matthew had left the couch and had been playing in the room while Bobby and I were in the bathroom. For the first time, he seemed shocked, but only because the commotion had disturbed his play. I was motionless on the floor. I heard Matthew grab some toys and leave the room at Bobby's order.

Debbie came rushing into the room screaming. Bobby warned her to leave, but I could see her clinging to him as she had before. He dragged her limply as he advanced toward me, shaking his arms free with ease.

"Dis mufucka done threw up piss and shit all ova' me after he done pissed all ova' da floor. Dis mufucka need to learn him a lesson an' I gonna teach him. I told ya'll ta quit fuckin' wit' me and

dis time he gon' pay!" His last word was drawn out as he grabbed my feet and dragged me to the window.

"You don' eva' learn nothin'. Today you gon' learn boy." He dragged me to the far right window and dropped my feet to the floor. He opened the window and hoisted me up by my belt loop. He draped my upper body onto the windowsill, grabbing my ankles and shoving the rest of my body out window. He held my limp body out of the third story window, my back against the outer wall of the building. I looked up to see Debbie crying in the left window. Bobby yelled at me from the window, but I didn't pay attention. I hoped he would drop me. I wanted him to kill me so it would all be over. This life was not life, I thought. As I hung there, I threw up again. My nose filled with a mix of bile and urine that also stung my eyes closed. I banged my head against the building trying to clear my nose, as I wiped my eyes.

The left window opened, and I saw Debbie reaching down. She grabbed my arms, and I stretched in her direction. With a firm hold of my arms, Debbie pulled me toward her as Bobby laughed and let me hang from my ankles. My short chubby body was stretched across the thin sill. Bobby and Debbie argued while Debbie's grip on my upper body strengthened. She wrapped her arms around my chest and pulled me away from Bobby who had loosened his grip. Debbie fell backward into the room. My urine and vomit soaked body on top of her, she sat up and wiped my face with her shirt. I coughed and blew my nose clear. Bobby chortled as he stood, then called for Matthew. Matthew appeared in the doorway with his hands full of toys.

"Matt, go grab yo daddy a beer and bring it to my room," was all he said as he turned to leave. Matthew dropped his toys eagerly and left the room first. Debbie sat on the floor rocking my battered body in her arms.

Chapter Fifteen
Third Shift

My shifts at the JDC changed when I went full-time. I started working Wednesday through Sunday, instead of just weekends. The County was doing away with part-time employees, so I had a choice to make: work full-time or quit. Since I was already working so much, I thought I could work full-time at school during the day and then go to the JDC at night. The Captain made a concession for me and let me work second shifts until school let out, then I would start a second and third swing shift schedule. In the meantime, my Sunday morning shift was changed to a Sunday night shift. While I felt confident and competent in my skills on the job, my full understanding of the scope of responsibilities at the JDC started with a favor for a co-worker. I had only worked first and second shifts on weekends, and I knew that Monday through Friday (first shift) was an experience I would

never have because of my teaching commitment during the day at school. One night, another officer asked me if I would work one of his third shifts in place of one of my second shifts. Not thinking any further than the fact that I would have a Friday night off to spend with my girlfriend for the first time in months, I agreed. The third shift he needed happened to fall on a three-day weekend from school, so it would be easy for me to do without compromising sleep or school.

We agreed to swap my Friday night second shift for his Sunday night third, requiring us both to work double shifts. Looking forward to a Friday night date with my girlfriend clouded my mind as I made the swap. Additionally, I had stayed up all night plenty of times, even in my adult life, without any physical repercussions. I knew my body could handle it. What I wasn't expecting was the drastic change of atmosphere and environment that existed on third shift.

The Sunday evening shift went on without incident. I had been working at the JDC for several months, and I had my own routine and felt more comfortable than ever. When midnight arrived, I was still feeling pretty good about the next eight hours that I had in front of me. The only unknown I could think of was the people on the shift. Tre was on that shift, but aside from him, I only knew the others in passing. I had met them all, but it was always as they were walking in, and I was heading home with my mind on the fresh air of freedom. The Sergeant and I had spoken only briefly, but I knew quite a bit about him. He was a family man, about my age. He had a wife and a couple of kids, and by all accounts was an all-around great guy. He also worked alongside the officers under his command. If for nothing else, I respected him for this fact, being a firm believer in not ever asking someone to do something that I was not willing to do myself. This work ethic went very far with my students.

My first third shift started out smoothly. The night had been quiet leading into it, and we were fully staffed, so the workload was going to be light if we didn't get too many new arrivals. I started on some laundry, one of the main tasks of third shift, and ran the first set of clocks to get them out of the way. Then I sat down with Tre and Sergeant Henley, who insisted I call him by his first name, Garland. They were discussing sports, which I know very little about, so I just listened. Somewhere in the middle of it all, I jumped into the conversation, and we spent our time between loads of laundry getting to know each other. There's not a whole lot to keep you awake on third shift in the Detention Center, other than the people you were working with. On subsequent shifts, I tried reading, but nearly always fought to stay awake. Talking kept us awake, and talk we did.

Though I had never spoken to Garland before, he asked the same questions I had answered so many

times before about teaching and working at the JDC. He was a very easy person to talk to, so when he asked why I would choose to work there after teaching all day, I gave him an honest answer--the most honest answer I had given anyone who had asked me that same question. "I've been a bad person for a long time. I've hurt a lot of bad people, but I've also hurt a lot of good people. So here I am trying to do what I can to make up for everything I've done by helping other people. I am the teacher I needed when I was a kid. If I had a teacher like me when I was young, I wouldn't have made all the mistakes I made to learn what I know. I had no guidance, no discipline, and no interest for anything outside of myself." I said in an unrestrained stream of consciousness.

"What do you mean you've been a bad person? You might *have done* some bad things but that does not make you a bad person. These kids love you. They talk about you all the time. And they talk

about you with respect. They're always asking if you're coming in so they can talk with you." Garland said quickly.

"Before I came to Tennessee, I was into some shit I'm not proud of, and before all of that some things happened that just made me into a very angry person. Now I'm trying to work through those things by helping these kids." I found myself feeling defensive.

"Well then, there had to be something that made you change, something that put you on this path. How did you get here? How you end up doing what you do?" He asked.

"To make a long story boring, when I got to Tennessee I went to the university and tried to be a tutor but found that all of those jobs went to graduate students. So as I left the building, I saw this sign that said 'Free Rent. Get Paid.' I copied the address, went and bought a map, went to the place, and the next thing I know I'm living in a house with two men with mental retardation and

taking care of them while I was going to college. I did that for five years. I had originally wanted to be an art teacher, but working with those guys made me realize that I had a compassion and patience that I never realized I had. So I went into special education. Then I found out that there were classes for kids with behavior and emotional problems, so I decided to do that, or try to teach in a juvenile detention center."

"See man, you're carrying all this anger around, but just sitting here listening to you tell that I story I can't help but think that there's some sort of plan or a path that you are on that's leading you to your calling. Now, I don't want to get into a discussion about religion with you, but did you ever wonder why we go through what we go through? We all go through certain situations that we have to find a way to handle it, and then we'll be put in a position to help other people." He noted all of this casually.

"Man, you know, now that you bring up religion, I had this thought one time. I went to go see that movie 'Passion of the Christ' and there's the scene where he's getting whipped but he keeps getting back up. Not like Rocky or something, but he gets up again and again, to take the pain and it's supposed to be some allegory. Everyone in the theater was crying all around me, but all I could think of was my students. I took all this abuse as a kid and survived all of this shit, excuse my language, but I did all that and kept getting back up. I wouldn't let it get me down even though it hurt. Sure I carry it around, but I use it to help my kids. Now, I am in no way comparing myself to the Christ, but at that moment, that's all I could think of." I surprised myself by speaking these words out loud.

"That's what I'm taking about," Garland continued, "You took that moment to reflect while everyone else was into the movie. Most people don't think that way, but what you have to

think about in that same sense is once that scene was over and Christ was nailed to the cross - that burden was lifted. You need to let that burden go!" His emphasis and message were clear. I excused myself to get some laundry. In the laundry room I wrote down what he had said and stuffed my notes in my pocket. I returned with a basket of laundry, and we continued talking as we folded.

"Man, I'm not comparing myself to you in any way cuz I was never abused, physically or sexually, but I was drug through the mud mentally. My dad left when I was two years old. My grandmother raised me. I came out here, like you did, to get away from it all. Then my dad tried to come back into my life when I was making a name for myself in football. But then I ended up not playing ball my junior year in college because of something my mother did. She went about her ways and kept on doing her thing. I was the one that was hurting. I carried a lot of

anger toward my mother for a lot of years. I went a whole year without seeing my mom. Sitting here, I see me in you. We're just two guys that had some stuff that went on in the past and it just so happened that I was able to lay it to bed while you're still carrying it around. You are not responsible for these kids in here. You aren't responsible for the kids in your classes. You can't walk around everyday thinking you have to make up for the past. You can only do what you can do in the present to make your own life better, and if you make other lives better in the process, like you're doing, then that's even better." He spoke to me like I speak to my kids, but also like psychiatrist and counselors had spoken to me for years, but coming from a peer it came across more sincerely. His words broke through me. Sitting there I felt as if he could see through me and see the baggage I carried, and he understood. Our conversation went on like this for hours, comparing notes with each other about people we

had hurt and the reckless lifestyles we had lived before turning our lives around. Tre would interject here and there, but it was mainly Garland and me having the most honest conversation I'd had in a long time. Talking to him was emotionally exhausting, but I felt refreshed and energized at the same time. By his tone and manner, I could tell that Garland understood what I was saying in a way no other person had before. My spirit felt renewed much like when I left my counselor's office after our therapy sessions.

The conversation was somehow more real than a therapy session because, as we talked all night, we mopped, cleaned, and folded laundry. Working side by side with this wise, insightful man made his words take on more meaning than he could have imagined. And his words kept coming at me. There was an urgency in his message to me, just as there was an urgency in my message to the kids.

"You don't owe anyone anything. You can't walk around with this burden on your shoulders, carrying the weight of your past. You have no one you have to do right by except yourself. I learned that the hard way, as I'm sure you have too. I'm sure you know all this stuff I'm saying; you just have to put it into action. When I put my anger aside and forgave my people, I decided I was going to be a positive light for other people. We all just gotta try to find our way." His words rang true in me, and I excused myself again to run to the bathroom to take more notes.

I never told Garland how much his words meant to me, or how they changed me. When I emerged from the bathroom with my pocket full of notes, it was nearly six in the morning. It was time, I was told, to get the guys ready for their showers. I had taken plenty of new detainees for their intake shower, but I had never done morning showers before. This experience made me realize that I

did not have the full understanding of the job that I had thought I had.

Morning showers consisted of waking up the block before breakfast to let each detainee take a shower. Each block had two showers in one large shower stall located at the top of the block. The shower stall was separated by a curtain hung about six feet off the ground and was just large enough to provide privacy from the person next to you. There was no privacy from the staff member assigned to watch. Staff were required to monitor showers because some kids would not use soap, others would not use deodorant, some would stand by the running water but not step into the shower at all. I discovered all of these tendencies that first morning.

With Sergeant Henley's words racing through my mind, I flipped the light switch at the top of the block. The florescent lights flickered on, slowly, but blindingly, illuminating the block. I walked through the small corridor behind the showers to

turn the water on. Both showerheads erupted with loud, powerful streams, as I pulled the ball valves open. The detainees had no control over the temperature, pressure, or direction of the water. The ancient steel door slammed, despite my best efforts to close it gently. If the water hadn't woken the guys, I was sure the echo of the slamming door had. I was wrong. Being in Detention for long stretches had made most of the detainees immune to the noises of the building, just as the constant noises of the building had become nothing but white noise to me. I walked the block announcing "Shower Time" in a conciliatory tone. The boys woke wearily and began to sit up on their bunks, as I made my way back up the block continually announcing "Shower Time" in my kindest tone. I opened the first cell, and two half-awake young men emerged, shivering in their underwear. They walked up the frigid block in their underwear and Detention Center-issued flip-flops. One had

another pair of underwear in his hand, the other shuffled behind him empty-handed. I greeted them with a quiet, "Good morning gentlemen," and they responded with equal respect. They stepped forward and undressed before me. I stepped to the side, trying to give them as much privacy as was allowed.

Not having been shown how to ready an entire block of 12 to 18 boys for showers, I did my best. I brought warm towels straight from the dryer and hung them on the single wall of bars that surrounded the shower stall, creating a secondary curtain between the kids and myself. I placed an empty clothes hamper on the floor to catch the used towels. Before each set of guys came to the showers, I placed a clean towel on the safety rail on the wall just outside each shower stall, and a can of spray deodorant just below. In the center of the showers, I placed a large bottle of lotion. The lotion and deodorant were normally kept in the lock box.

The guys came up the block and showered quickly and quietly. Some had to be directed to use soap or deodorant, but before I knew it, I had completed showers for the first block. Some of the boys came up the block more awake than others, and they strolled up the block half-naked, without any visible sign of self-consciousness. However, the guys that had been students in school walked up the block with their heads down and passed me in conspicuous shame, as our two worlds of school and Detention collided.

The next block of showers also occurred without incident, but the kids were more awake, having been woken by the opening and closing of the cells on the opposite block. Being more awake, the guys on the second block thanked me for their warm towels and for the deodorant and lotion already being set out for them. Again, the guys that I had taught in school walked up the block with their heads down without making eye contact with me throughout the shower process.

When the showers were complete, it was time for breakfast. Another officer and I passed out the trays of food. The guys started to make the connection that I had been there since the night before, and many of them called me crazy for having been there all night, though many staff members pulled double shifts frequently. As their words sank in, Garland's words worked themselves deeper into my psyche. While I walked around collecting their empty breakfast trays, I gleefully laughed with the guys as they kidded me for working so much, asking if I had slept in one of the empty cells. As we joked, the 16-hour shift became a reality.

Descending the stairs, I could hear the buzzing of the secure doors. Before I could see them, I could hear the staff of first shift arriving and readying the morning's work assignments. I had never seen Monday morning first shift, and when I did I was amazed and overwhelmed by their manic furor, especially that of Officer Bobby Hall Jr. whose

whirlwind of activity seemed to energize the whole shift. Everyone was working in unison, preparing for court, school, transfers and transports, all experiences I was unfamiliar with. It was too much to take in with my mind still trained on my nightlong conversation with Garland and Tre. Watching the immediacy and efficiency of the first shift staff brought exhaustion washing over me, and suddenly I could not get out of the building fast enough. When at last I made my way outside, the sun blinded me after nearly a full day in the dank building. I tramped to my Jeep and climbed lazily into the seat, excited to be going home to the comforts of sleep, relaxation and later, reflection.

Chapter Sixteen
The Horror of Rescue

Debbie, Matthew and I were setting up the kitchen, eagerly awaiting Bobby's return. He was out on a big score. He had excited Debbie with promises of the money he was going to make, in addition to his promise that she would not have to work any more cold nights on the streets. Everything was laid out in the kitchen to divide the heroin into smaller, street-ready packages. The three of us had gone through this process many times for Bobby to shorten the time it took to get the dope to the people that would come over and buy the smaller, yet still large, packages from him. When the door opened, Bobby strutted pompously to the kitchen table and sat into the nearest chair. Dumping the package in the clear spot on the table, his pleasant attitude changed to one of irritation. He spread the brick-like bundles of heroin onto the table, scattering the prepared scales, powder, and bags onto the floor.

Something had gone wrong. As Bobby surveyed the bundles, he became increasingly furious and began to yell. Something was missing, he said. He had been shorted a large amount of dope. Standing up, he sent the cheap wooden chair crashing against the front door. Stomping to the phone just a few feet away, he cursed and threatened Debbie as she tried, in vain, to calm him. Within seconds of grabbing the phone, he spewed his rage through clenched teeth at the person on the other end, some middleman somewhere. He slammed the phone down and prowled the kitchen and living room in a menacing fury. Again Debbie spoke to him, attempting to calm his temper, but her words only seemed to further enrage him.

He picked me from the floor and threw me against the wall. I crumbled to the ground, my arms and legs splayed out. His fury was unleashed when he picked up the baseball bat that was always positioned by the front door. He grabbed

the bat and bashed my legs, chest, and finally my head before I was unconscious.

I was blind when I opened my eyes. The glare from the lights slowly faded, and I could make out shadowy forms. I heard voices, but I could make no sense of the words. I felt warm, wet lips against my ear.

"Can you hear me, honey?" The voice sang, "You're gonna be OK." I knew the voice. It was Bobby's sister, the woman we called Donna Summer. She was tall, elegant, and beautiful. We had seen her infrequently, but she was always kind and loving when she was with us.

She lifted me from my bed, and I screamed in pain. She continued her gentle reassurances, as she carried me from my room. I heard muffled voices, as we escaped from the apartment and down the stairs. Though she tried to hold me close, my battered body jostled in the young woman's arms, as we made our way through the cold stairwell. It was even colder, as I was placed

onto the back seat of an unfamiliar car. Debbie, several months pregnant, Matthew, Ruby, and I were shuttled to a local hospital. The ride was uncomfortable, and I cried most of the way until I fell asleep.

When I regained full consciousness, I was laid out on a hospital bed in the center of a long, bright hallway. Debbie and Matthew were also in beds close to me. My head was fixed to the bed, but I could see Debbie's bruised and swollen face several feet away. My vision was blurred, but I recognized the beaten face of my mother. Matthew was sitting in his bed, playing with a toy. I tried to reach out, but I could not move my hands or even my arms. I tried to move my legs, but immediately started to cry from the intense pain. In frustration and panic, I called for my mother. She spoke to me through swollen lips, and I heard her telling me, as she often did, that everything was going to be all right. Through my tears, I saw a young nurse appear over my

immobilized head. She told me everything was going to be fine, and she wiped my face. I saw the blood-soaked rag, as she wiped it back and forth across my face. My vision was clearing up, and I tried to talk to Debbie, whose bed was across the narrow hallway from me. She reached out for my bed and wrapped her thin, skeletal hand around my bedrail. She promised that I would be OK and that the pain would go away soon. She began to describe the medicine the doctors had given me, and how soon I wouldn't feel any pain. I wanted to yell at her in disbelief, but I knew not to yell at her. I didn't know where Bobby was, but I was sure he was close by. I was confused and light-headed. Unable to move my body, I was unable to speak clearly, unable to reach out for comfort, but watching Matthew playing on his bed – having a good time as usual. Staring at Debbie's slightly blurred face, I fell silently back into unconsciousness.

There were voices squabbling when I woke. I was in a private room with no sign of Debbie or Matthew. The two young nurses who stood at my feet bickered about something I didn't understand. They were using medical jargon that I had not yet become familiar with. Finally they approached my bed from opposing sides and stopped midway along the bedrail. They spoke to me in hushed tones, but their words were nearly inaudible. They told me about a catheter, but I did not know what they meant. The younger looking nurse pulled the pale blue sheet from my body and I saw my legs in casts extending beyond my knees. My surprise was short lived.

As I stared at my legs, the nurse pulled my thin papery hospital gown up, exposing my naked body to the chilly hospital air. With gloved hands, the two nurses attempted to insert a hard catheter. The pain was instant and intense. Bobby had often made sport of hurting this particular area of my body in his nearly incessant

attempts at my emasculation, but this was different. I squirmed and screamed, but there was no escaping. They tried to settle me down, but I wouldn't cooperate. Even when they explained that they were not trying to hurt, but to help me, I screamed and cursed them. After conceding defeat, I surrendered to their insistence. The pain was excruciating. The two had significant trouble inserting the catheter and it took a third person to come in and assist. Once the procedure was complete, I no longer felt pain or animosity toward the staff. I tried to apologize, but my cries overpowered my voice.

The nurses stayed and talked me through my tears. They tried to joke with me, but I insisted on detailing life with Bobby, and all of the terrifying sexual experiences I had endured living with Bobby. They listened long enough for me to feel better; then they all excused themselves, closed the curtain surrounding my bed, and turned the television volume higher. I lay there in my bed,

staring at the new apparatus extending from me. Every now and again one of the nurses that had been with me earlier came in to check on me, each one catching me playing with the long tube extending from me, and each one warning me against playing with it. After learning the hard way that trying to pull it out was as painful as when it had been put in, I finally left it alone. I stayed in the bed for some time before seeing Debbie or Matthew again. While I remained strapped to the bed, most of my body cast in plaster, they both came to visit me to tell me they were leaving the hospital. Debbie's face was still slightly bruised, but she looked healthy and more noticeably pregnant than I remembered. Matthew ran around and played in my room until he noticed the tube coming from beneath my gown. After explaining to him what it was, he cringed momentarily, but then laughed. His laughter made me flush with anger, then jealousy, as I watched him bend over with joy. I wanted to

be free from the restraints of the bed. I wanted to walk around, but I never wanted to go home. In a very short period of time, I had developed a sense of calm within the hospital.

The hospital staff paid a lot of attention to me; even though sometimes it hurt, it felt nice to be taken care of by such gentle and caring people. The parts of my body that were exposed were softly sponged clean each day. Every couple of days a nurse would come in with a couple of scrub sponges. The sponges came in shiny silver airtight packages that we would squeeze open and make them pop. The popping sound always made me laugh, and it was the lead in to the circus of distraction she used to allow my mind to ignore the scrubbing of the scabs from the multiple infections on my exposed skin. After she would let me pop one open, and squeeze it until the soap suds appeared, I'd scrub my hands and fingernails like I'd watched the hospital staff do so often before they touched me. The sponges had short

rubbery bristles on one side that the nurse would use to scrub the scab away from my infected wounds. The other side of the sponge was a scouring pad with which she would tenderly clean out the exposed skin more thoroughly. Her sympathetic attention was obvious as she winced each time she began. It seemed to pain her more than me, though I was too busy scrubbing my hands and playing doctor to notice any pain. Additionally, the hospital was a much more pleasant environment than life with Bobby, and the pain of my body healing was much easier to bear than the pain of the beatings that got me there.

Throughout my extended stay in the hospital, I watched a lot of television. I had never been allowed to watch much television when Bobby was around, and having unlimited access to my own television was thrilling. Life with Bobby and Debbie had never afforded the luxury of a stable sleep pattern, so even medicated I had trouble

staying asleep throughout the night. Though the medications made me sleep odd hours, I became a faithful fan of prime time programming, especially *Charlie's Angels*, *Buck Rogers*, *CHiPs*, *Fantasy Island* and *Love Boat*. It was never a problem getting the staff to change channels for me. Everyone that stopped by was eager to make me happy. The staff brought me snacks, magazines, and comic books. In the middle of the night, I would talk to doctors, nurses and orderlies just to pass the time.

One day I got a visit from someone who did not work at the hospital. She was tall, dark haired, and soft-spoken. She introduced herself, but I did not pay attention to her name. I was young, but since being introduced to sexual activity I had an uncommon awareness of and attraction to beautiful women. Staring at her brought me into my new fantasy world of loving Kelly Garrett from *Charlie's Angels*. In my mind this stranger and I lived happily ever after, until she said the words

"protective custody". Instantly I was back in my hospital bed talking to a social worker. I had heard the words protective custody before. Several times during our visits to the welfare offices, Debbie had been threatened with protective custody. After Matthew's dalliance into foster care, I came to have a better understanding of what the words really meant. She didn't say where we were going, but she promised me that I would not be going back to the Village. The statuesque woman lulled me back into my fantasy family life, as she spoke of taking me with her as soon as I could leave the hospital. All of a sudden, leaving the spoiling comforts of the hospital could not come soon enough. She left me with a quick kiss on the forehead and a promise to come back as soon as I was able to walk on my own. Standing and walking took on a new urgency now that I believed I was going home with one of *Charlie's Angels*. I had been ready to get out of the bed for some time, but every time I tried, the pain

was nearly unbearable. Meeting Karen, the new social worker, was all the motivation I needed. The nurse warned that I would feel a "little sting" as she eased the catheter out. The sting was more like a stabbing, as the seemingly endless tube was pulled free. I clenched the bedrails and did my best to keep my body still. With the casts off, the infections cleared, and cuts healed, the catheter was the last thing keeping me from being fully mobile. At the final tug the relief I felt was indescribable. After wiping my legs dry, my nurse lowered the bedrails and took my hands. She sat me up and coaxed me out of the bed. Having not used my legs much since the casts came off, the nurse lifted them gently and draped them over the side of the bed. I cried the moment my feet touched the ground, but with the nurse supporting my weight and steadying me as I went, I made it the few steps to the doorway and back again. Standing up and looking down the hallway was overwhelming. I was crying from the

pain, but also the joy, of walking. All of the staff in the hallway clapped, as I emerged into the stark white hall. I was embarrassed from the attention, and that everyone had seen me crying. The nurse quickly escorted me back into the room, where she eased me back into my bed. She didn't say anything as she left me crying quietly in my bed.

Days later, my room was half-filled with balloons for my "Going Home" party. I had cried my way through walking rehab, but after a few days and many trips back and forth to the bathroom I was told I was ready for discharge. Karen had been by several times encouraging me to get better, and with each visit I was more invigorated. Now it was time to leave all of my hospital friends, and I was more than ready to go home with Karen. During my stay in the hospital, I had been able to put all thoughts of living with Bobby, Debbie, and Matthew out of my mind. On her last visit, Karen told me she would be taking me to a foster home,

where I would live with Matthew and some other children. Until she mentioned Matthew's name, I had believed that Karen was taking me home to live with her. She may have mentioned foster care to me during an earlier visit, but since our first meeting, I had only thought of living with Karen. Matthew was waiting in the hall when I was wheeled out of my room in a wheel chair with all of my new clothes, toys, and magazines that the staff had brought for me packed into plastic bags on my lap. Though I had been walking on my own for a while, I was not allowed to walk out of the hospital. Seeing Matthew made me extraordinarily sad, as I left my peaceful room for the last time. His face brought my pre-hospital life clearly into focus in my mind. We looked at each other in silence, and he trotted alongside the beautiful Karen as she wheeled me out of the hospital.

Meeting the Mattisons in March of 1980 was a difficult experience. They were an older white

couple with a house full of foster children and a daughter of their own. The foster children were of all ages and races, except black. I felt very strange not seeing any black people around. The Village and the hospital were full of black folks, and I rarely saw other white people. Living in a nearly all-white house in an all-white neighborhood was very unnerving. I spent the first few weeks hiding in the bedroom I shared with Matthew. Hording the magazines and comics I had gotten from the hospital staff, I kept to myself and out of everyone's way . . . until I smelled marijuana.

One day, one of the other foster kids came upstairs reeking of marijuana. Though it had been months since I had smoked any, the minute I smelled it I wanted to get high. My fondest memories of Debbie were of the times we got high together. I followed the girl downstairs and into the kitchen where I eagerly asked the teenaged girl for a joint. Mr. Mattison overheard

my overt request and went ballistic. Though I thought nothing of it, the girl became very angry with me and denied being high.

Mr. Mattison ordered me upstairs, and he followed close behind as we climbed the steep stairway to his bedroom. He told me to drop my pants, and I became suspicious of his intentions. He pulled his belt from his pants, though not as quickly or easily as Bobby had. With his thin black belt, he beat my bare bottom several times. I could not help it when I started laughing. Though he was a large, heavy man, Mr. Mattison's lashes did not compare to the beatings I suffered from Bobby's iron-fist. As my laughter got louder Mr. Mattison was caught off-guard. He dropped his belt where he stood and ordered me to pull my pants up. He slapped me once across the face and called me crazy. Whether he meant I was crazy for asking for the joint or for laughing, he didn't clarify, but he mentioned them both in his flurry of reprimands. As I zipped

my pants, he ordered me to my room. I walked off confidently, but realizing I had a lot to learn about being in a "normal" family.

After a couple of months of "protective custody" at the Mattisons, Karen showed up at the house and told Matthew and I that we would have to go with her to court. She warned us that we would be seeing Debbie and Bobby, but that she would be there to protect us. Matthew cheered at the mention of seeing Debbie and Bobby. On May 23, 1980 she drove us to the courthouse on Golden Hill in Bridgeport. Debbie and Bobby were already waiting outside like a happy couple. Matthew ran to Bobby immediately. Bobby lifted him up and put him on his shoulders and walked him down to the edge of the street and bought him an ice cream from a street vendor. Making his way over to Debbie and me, Bobby looked as mean as I remembered. He bent down with Matthew still perched on his shoulders. He spoke

to me quietly, but loud enough for Debbie to hear.

"You gonna get in there and tell deez people that yo mother did all dis shit to you. If you say anything else I'm gonna kill all a'ya. Ya undastan?" He growled. I understood that his threat was real, and I knew what I had to do. I nodded my head and clung to Debbie's leg, as she gripped me tightly around the shoulders. She looked down at me and told me to do as I was told. Bobby put Matthew down on the ground, and the four of us walked up the stairs to the courthouse, Matthew still happily eating his ice cream.

We waited in a hall for a while, as Matthew finished his ice cream. After some time, Matthew and I were escorted into the judge's chambers by a bailiff. We were seated directly in front of a judge where we were to testify. The judge explained the process and asked Matthew several questions. He answered honestly, which he could

do since he had never been hit. When it was my turn to speak, I told the judge exactly what Bobby had told me to say. The judge listened intently and dismissed Matthew and I as soon as I was done talking.

We were allowed to hug Debbie one last time before the bailiff took her away. Matthew hugged Bobby as I stood beside Karen waiting anxiously to leave. On the ride back to the Mattison's, the guilt of sending my mother to prison began to set in, though I knew I had saved her life, and my own. For the first time I felt at peace, knowing I would never have to see Bobby again.

Chapter Seventeen
The Letter and the Call

"Last night I told my sister I was going to kill her father," I thought to myself. The words rang in my head, as I stood in front of my students. Had I made a mistake? Would she talk to me again? How would I get through to her? How would I get through this day? My heart pounded, and I felt myself beginning to sweat, despite the 60 some-odd degree temperature of my classroom. As I stood before my students, my brain raced, and I was having trouble focusing.

"Guys, go ahead and open your laptops and type this into your search browser." It was a simple instruction. I turned to the white board and wrote a few words. With my back to the class, I instructed the boys to read what I was writing on the board.

"Type in CT DOC inmate search," my face was getting warm, and I wondered if they could sense my anxiety.

"Go ahead and hit enter. Now click on the first item that appears. Now type in this number in the box that says Inmate Number, and hit enter." I looked down at the envelope in my hand and read the number from the return address to the boys, sitting attentively in front of me.

"Now click on the blue number. " I looked up at the boys, as they read the page displayed on their screens.

"What you're looking at is the Connecticut Department of Corrections information on my brother. A brother I've never met and have never had contact with until yesterday." With my trademark honesty, I told the boys about my search for my brother and the letter I had written him a few weeks earlier during our weekly letter-writing activity.

"I wrote a very simple letter explaining who I am, what I do, and where I've been. I sent him one of the few pictures I have of my biological mother to prove that I am who I said I am. I didn't expect

to get a response, but in case I did, I used the school address--just to be on the safe side."
Taking a deep breath, I held fast to the letter in my hand and continued.

"Well, yesterday afternoon I got a letter from him. When I went to my mailbox in the office, I saw the letter and nearly fell over. I reached in and felt it and realized that it was much more than the one sentence response of 'leave me alone' that I had expected." I took another deep breath and looked out to see the captivated faces in front of me. They expressed more rapt attention than I had ever witnessed from them before.

"I sat at my desk and read the letter, and when I was done I let the letter fall from my hands, and I nearly threw up. Here was this person I had never met, but after reading the letter, I felt like I was reading something I would have written when I was twelve. This man and I had shared so much in our lives, and yet our paths had not

crossed. In his letter he wrote that our sister, who I haven't seen since 1995, was living in Delaware. So I googled her name and Delaware and sure enough her name, address and phone number popped up. So I called her. I left a message and put the phone down and re-read the letter."

I looked from face to face, trying to keep my wits about me, as I told these lost children my own story of being a lost child.

"A few minutes later my phone rang, and the voice on the other end said my name. I asked who it was, and she said 'It's Ruby.' I asked her what had been the last thing we had done together, and she replied quickly, 'We went shopping,' and I knew that this was my sister. We talked for a long time, and I told her the abbreviated version of what I'd been doing since I'd last seen her. She told me her own story, and she told me about being at our mother's side when she had died. Throughout the conversation, I noticed that she also did not refer to Debbie as

mom or mother or any of those words. Just like I
do, she referred to our mother by her name,
Debbie. Then we talked about her father. In my
random stream of speech, I told her that all of the
horrifying experiences I had with her father had
made me the man I am today. Then she said
something that I will never forget. Now, this is a
grown woman with two kids, living on her own,
far from any family. She said to me 'my father
made *me* the man that I am' and I knew exactly
what she meant."

The boys were entranced by the story, and I
knew I had to go on. We talked for nearly 30
minutes about their own estrangement from
family members and how they would like to find
their own brothers, sisters, mothers, and/or
fathers one day, each young man telling his own
heart-breaking story.

I told the boys that I was having very hard time
keeping my mind focused. "I am a little
overwhelmed right now, and I was worse last

night. My brain would not shut off last night, and I was up far too late thinking about all of these new developments in my 'family' relationships." As I stood in front of them, I was excessively tired and absent-minded. "All I ask of you is to give me a little time to collect my thoughts, get my brain together, and I'll be good. If you guys do what you need to do this morning," I always give my students the week's lesson plans on Monday so they know what's expected each hour of each day, "I'm gonna do some paperwork and try to get my mind where it needs to be, and we'll pick it up in a little bit. Is that cool?" I asked, trying not to sound too desperate.

"Yes Sir," the boys said in a calm, collective voice.

"Thank you. You all have your assignments. Let me know if you need any help." I walked to my desk. Before I could get started in on some long over-due and all-consuming paperwork, one of my boys raised his hand.

"Mr. Love, can I talk to you outside for a second?" Scott asked.

"Of course Sir." I answered as I got up and headed for the back door with the young man following me. When the door closed, the young man began fidgeting with his hands, held his head down for a moment, and then took a deep breath. "Does every state have one of those inmate look-up things?" He asked.

"I believe so. I haven't checked all 50, but I have used inmate searches in a bunch of them, and I've never had a problem." I answered honestly.

"Sir, my dad molested my sister and I when we were kids, and he's supposed to be locked up somewhere. I don't know where or if he's still locked up. Do you think I could find him online? I'm always afraid that he's gonna come and find me and try to hurt me again. That's why my mom and I move all the time." He spoke with a mixture of sadness and confidence that made his story believable. His behaviors that brought him

to me included a lot of bizarre sexual acting out which is indicative of a child that has been sexually abused, so his admission was not surprising.

We spoke for a few minutes, and I explained how he could look up his father. He told me that his sister had been taken out of the home and placed into foster care, and that he hadn't seen her in several years and how much it pained him to not know anything about her. He did not know that I was already aware that his sister had been removed from the home years before, but his explanation made the story I had been told come together to form a more clear family history.

"I go to therapy every week, but I never tell them anything about how I really feel." He confessed, "I don't want my mom to know that I miss my sister because I know it bothers her too, and I don't want to cause her any more problems. I'm afraid that if I tell the shrink something like that she'll tell my mom and my mom will get mad."

"Well Sir, I have to tell you from experience, that therapy is never easy, but the first thing you need to do is to be honest. No matter how much it hurts, you have to be honest. I went to therapy for nearly 10 years and I was never honest. I told the doctors what I thought they wanted to hear just so I could get out of their offices. Then I got old, and it all caught up with me. Now I go to therapy and I'm honest, and I feel like a new person every time I leave the office because I leave all the crap I talk about *in the office*. I really cannot express to you how great that feels. I really do feel like a new person." I did my best to convey my sincerity as I spoke. "If you start being honest, you're mom will have a better understanding of what's going on with you and how she can help you. Because right now I'm sure she's blaming herself for what you're doing and what you're going through."

"Maybe I should be honest," he said looking sadly, "I just don't want to hurt my mom, Mr. Love."

"Sir, to be honest, you're hurting your mom *now* with your lies and sneaking around. You might want to start there," I recommended. His eyes began to tear up as my words sunk in. Trying to give him a way out, I put my hand on his shoulder and asked if he was ready to go inside. He hesitated and then threw his arms around me in a bear hug.

With his face buried in my sleeve I heard him say, "Thank you Sir." Stunned by the sudden show of emotion from this normally stoic young man, I stood firm and let him have his moment. He released his grip and stood back, wiping his eyes.

"You cool?" I asked, trying to maintain my own emotions.

"Yes Sir, thank you Sir." He said as I reached for the door. Before I could open the door he called my name. I stopped and looked at him. He

cleared his throat and said, "Thank you for being so honest with us. I appreciate it."

"Sir, if I wasn't honest with you I wouldn't be being honest with myself. I appreciate you guys too. Let's get back to work." I opened the door, and we went to our desks and got to work on our own projects.

Keeping my mind trained on my paperwork and not talking for a while had settled my mind. When I felt more together, I got up and took my position at the front of the room. I asked for status reports, and everyone told me where in their lessons they were working. I applauded their efforts and told them all to take a break. Scott came to my desk holding his laptop. He showed me the screen with his father's name prominently displayed on a Department of Corrections website. Whispering that he had found his father and he was glad to know where he was, he thanked me again and went to his seat. Scott's relief was evident and inspiring.

"Guys I want to share something with you. I told you this morning about the letter and the call from yesterday, but I want to help you understand why I'm doing all of this." I spoke as they closed their books and computers and settled into their seats.

"Guys, first I want to thank you for giving me the last hour to get my mind clear, in addition to getting some paperwork done. Secondly, I want to share a little of what I've been doing with you since we missed our Social Skills lesson for this morning. As you know I'm writing a book, and Scott asked if I would give copies to all of you when I was done, and I said that probably wasn't going to happen because of the content of the book. But that got me thinking, and I've tried to tone down as much as I could to make it so maybe there would be parts that you could read." I stood in front of them as I spoke.

"I've been working on a chapter, and I finished it last night, and right now it has one cuss word in

it, and it's not bad, so I thought I would share this one chapter with you. Do any of you want to hear it?" I teased. Every hand in the room shot up in agreement. I strolled to my book bag and pulled out a copy of the chapter that I had been proofing, and returned to the front of the room. I grabbed a free chair, spun it around, and started reading a chapter entitled "My Bodyguard". The guys responded well, and when it was over they gave me a standing ovation. David asked if it was true, and I told him it was absolutely true, except for the people's names, which I had to change. Another student, Kevin, raised his hand and asked, "Mr. Love, you wrote that? Cuz that sounds like a *real* book." He was serious, and we all knew it. The class exploded in laughter, including Kevin, though, when he laughed for a few seconds, he asked, "What?" with a dazed look on his face. The other boys assured him that I had written it, and we were laughing at and with

him. Kevin finally got the joke and laughed again. This made us all laugh harder still.

After the laughter died down, I told them everything I had learned about research over the course of writing my book. Though I had mentioned it to them before, the idea of writing a book became real to them after reading a chapter, and then showing them some of the old court documents I happened to have in my book bag. I told them about researching my family background, talking to different people at various newspapers, police departments, courts and hospitals trying to get vital records in order to get all of my details right. While they were impressed that I was *really* writing a book, the guys were most impressed when I gave real world examples of having used all of the resources I had taught them to use.

Speaking with my students about my research and writing allowed me to detach from it all. It became an academic issue, and I was able to

speak to my students as a teacher discussing research techniques; my brain clicked into that familiar and comfortable teaching mode. My anxiety lifted, and the kids brought me back to our reality, the reality that we had made with and for each other. Soon the day was rolling along, and we all got through it together, just as we always do.

Printed in the United States
147239LV00001B/4/P